2/02

synaesthesia
THE STRANGEST THING

synaesthesia
THE STRANGEST THING

john harrison

Principal Consultant, Cambridge
Psychometric Consultants & Honorary
Research Psychologist at the
Radcliffe Infirmary, Oxford

OXFORD
UNIVERSITY PRESS

OXFORD
UNIVERSITY PRESS

Great Clarendon Street, Oxford OX2 6DP

Oxford University Press is a department of the University of Oxford.
It furthers the University's objective of excellence in research, scholarship,
and education by publishing worldwide in

Oxford New York

Athens Auckland Bangkok Bogotá Buenos Aires Calcutta
Cape Town Chennai Dar es Salaam Delhi Florence Hong Kong
Istanbul Karachi Kuala Lumpur Madrid Melbourne Mexico City Mumbai
Nairobi Paris São Paulo Shanghai Singapore Taipei Tokyo Toronto Warsaw

with associated companies in Berlin Ibadan

Oxford is a registered trade mark of Oxford University Press
in the UK and in certain other countries

Published in the United States
By Oxford University Press Inc., New York

A catalogue record for this book is available from the British Library

Library of Congress Cataloguing in Publication Data

Harrison, John E.
Synaesthesia: the strangest thing/John Harrison.
p. cm.
Includes bibliographical references.
1. Synesthesia. I. Title
RC394 S93 H37 2001   616.8—dc21   00-067603

ISBN 0 19 263245 0

Typeset in Minion by EXPO Holdings, Malaysia
Printed in Great Britain
on acid-free paper by Biddles Ltd, Guildford & King's Lynn

Contents

Foreword

This book is very timely. When John Harrison and I began a collaborative investigation into synaesthesia in the 1990s the topic was still very controversial. The majority of neuroscientists were unwilling to take seriously the phenomenon, or the implications it has for scientific understanding. This was because the evidence base was still thin. A decade later and the situation has changed considerably, because the evidence is beginning to accumulate.

John Harrison has produced a scholarly yet accessible account of both the history and science of synaesthesia, and is even-handed in his treatment of the different theories that have attempted to explain it. He conveys the excitement of the researcher on the trail to new discoveries, and this is contagious. The hope is that this book will inspire the next generation of scientists to take up the challenge of learning more about this fascinating psychological and neurological state.

The author recognizes that studies of atypicality can shed light on typical function, and his approach to writing about this topic reveals how he is as much concerned to understand why some individuals have the gift of synaesthesia as to understand why the rest of us lack this gift: why our perception appears modular.

Aside from inspiring fellow researchers, this book will do much to educate the general public about the important but often overlooked point that we do not all experience this universe in the same way. I predict that this book will not only raise awareness that synaesthesia exists, but also set an important atmosphere of tolerance of differences, so that synaesthetes do not feel any stigma of abnormality or that they have a medical condition. On the contrary, their perception is simply different to others', and many would say richer. It is fortunately only rarely that forms of synaesthesia produce any discomfort (and it is from such rare forms that we may learn why it is important for the senses to remain very separate sometimes). For the most part, synaesthetes would not wish to be free of their synaesthesia and, if anything, feel somewhat sorry for the rest of us as we go about our unisensual existence. My guess also is that this valuable book will ring a colourful bell for many people who until now did not realize that their experience had a name, and who will now be able to identify themselves with like-minded others. For all these reasons, this is quite a book.

We should keep in mind that although significant steps have been made in understanding synaesthesia, a decade or two is a mere blink of an eye in the history of any science. We look forward to the new discoveries in our understanding that John Harrison's book will catalyse.

Simon Baron-Cohen
Cambridge University
Departments of Experimental Psychology and
Psychiatry
Downing Street
Cambridge CB2 3EB
UK

Acknowledgements

Ten years ago I was afforded the opportunity to become involved in research into synaesthesia, a condition that at the time was regarded as 'romantic neurology'. Often the condition needed explaining, what on earth was synaesthesia? Ten years on it is gratifying to meet neuroscientists and members of the public who know about the condition. One reason for this change has been the coverage given to research on synaesthesia by the press, radio, television and multimedia. This coverage has been extremely useful to us as it has encouraged synaesthetes to contact us and, in many cases, to assist us with our research. This mass of individuals now has the opportunity to discuss the condition with fellow synaesthetes through the auspices of the International Synaesthesia Assocation (ISA). In writing this book I have an excellent opportunity to extend my heartfelt thanks for their willingness to share their experiences with us. Thank you to you all.

The book has essentially a chronological structure to it, starting in the mists of time and ending in the present and near future. It is fortunate that our research shifted in emphasis from methodology to methodology throughout this period as this has made it possible for me to deal with a different facet of our work in each chapter without having to bend the course of time's arrow. This means that the book begins with historical concepts and then moves to psychological single case studies and group studies. The psychology then gives way to the anatomy (the study of areas), which in turn gives way to the physiology (the study of connections). The areas and their connections, both with each other and with behaviour, are discussed towards the end of the book, together with the genetic influences that may determine the way in which the connections are made.

I have several intentions for this book. It is first and foremost a book about synaesthesia. However, it is also something of a technical manual and I have sought to include some explanation of the various methods that were adopted during our investigations. Adding this aspect to the book should give the interested lay reader a grasp of technologies currently available to neuroscientists. I have also included snippets of interesting information. The books I have most enjoyed reading have been ones that often cause me to comment mentally, 'That's interesting' or 'Well, I never knew that'. I hope the reader will experience similar mental events at least once in reading this book. I have also included snippets of information best described as 'things I wish I had known sooner'. This particularly alludes to my career in neuroscience and may therefore be of particular use to those embarking on a course of study in psychology or neuroscience. Hopefully others will also benefit from the mention of these tidbits.

This preface is also an excellent opportunity to thank those with whom I have worked during the last decade. First and foremost I must thank Simon Baron-Cohen for introducing me to synaesthesia and synaesthetes during the summer of 1989. I found Simon's guidance both inspiring and thought-provoking and often had cause to admire his industriousness and clarity of thought. I have not until now had the opportunity to express my gratitude to him fully and to acknowledge the impact he has had upon the science of synaesthesia. Working for Simon and Dr Laura Goldstein during my placement at the Institute of Psychiatry was just the beginning of a string of good fortune for me. From 1989 until 1999 I was fortunate to have the chance to work and interact with some of the most distinguished minds in British neuroscience. A complete list would by now be impossible to compile, but it would be remiss of me not to thank some of those individuals by name. Whilst at the Royal London Hospital I had the immense good fortune to benefit from the guidance and wisdom of my PhD supervisors, Professor Leslie Henderson, Professor Christopher Kennard and Dr Susan Goodrich. Leslie in particular showed immense good cheer and patience with me, which must have been hard to do from time-to-time. He remains the individual to whom I am scientifically most indebted. Dr Christian Lueck and Malcolm Hawken also provided sources of encouragement and stimulation during my time at the Royal London. Later, at Charing Cross & Westminster Medical School, I benefited from working with a distinguished group of scientists. Amongst that group, special thanks must go to Dr Eileen Joyce, Dr Richard Wise, Dr Liz Warburton, Dr John Wade, Dr Donna Coleston and Mr Tim Matthews. My visiting Research Fellowship to the Medical Research Council's cyclotron unit at the Hammersmith Hospital again put me amongst the cream of British neuroscience. Special thanks to Professor Richard Frackowiak, Professor David Brooks, Professor Chris Frith, Professor Semir Zeki, Dr Eraldo Paulesu, Dr Cathy Price and Dr Harry Jenkins. Thanks also to all the radiographers who made the long hours of scanning so much fun.

During my time at the University of Cambridge, while working for the excellent Dr Patrick Bolton, I had the very good fortune to work with a number of helpful and know-ledgeable individuals. Thanks then to Professor Ian Goodyer, Professor Trevor Robbins, Dr Barbara Sahakian, Dr Adrian Owen and Dr Joanna Iddon. Others I must thank are Professor Steve Williams, Professor Ian MacDonald, Professor Jeffrey Gray, Dr Richard Cytowic and Alison Motluk. I would also be remiss if I failed to thank the many friends and colleagues who suffered the ordeal of reading and commenting on previous drafts of this book. For this I would like additionally to thank Helena Glenn and Simon Coggins.

Finally, thanks beyond expression to my wife Rachel for her patience and to my daughter Cordelia for her inspiration.

J.H.

Ely

June 2000

In science, take the strangest thing and
explore it thoroughly

CHAPTER 1

Confessions of a physicalist

A tactile dinner party

For the vast majority of us sensation is neatly divided into touch, vision, hearing, taste and smell – the five senses. However, in various fields of artistic endeavour there seem to have been attempts to bring these sensations together. The artist Kandinsky, for example, sought to imbue his canvasses with a sound dimension ('Klangen'), and composers such as Scriabin have deliberately sought to create a visual impression through their music. Perhaps a good example of this was Richard Wagner's (1813–1883) attempt to evoke the image of the river Rhine at the beginning of Das Rheingold. The 135 bars of E flat major were apparently inspired by the lapping motion of the waters of the Rhine that so infected the sleeping mind of the composer that he awoke with this theme, or *leitmotiv*, in his head ready to be committed to paper. Others have described deliciously fabulous and exotic methods for simultaneously arousing the senses. For example, the Italian futurist FT Marinetti (1876–1944) proposed the following tactile dinner party, to which guests were required to wear pyjamas 'made of, or covered with a different tactile material such as sponge, cork, sandpaper, felt, etc.' During the course of this dinner, the guests were invited to eat a 'tactile vegetable garden'. This was done by burying the face in the plate, without the help of the hands, so as to inspire a true tasting with direct contact between the flavours and textures of the green leaves on the skin and lips. Every time the diners raised their heads from the plate to chew, the waiters sprayed their faces with perfumes of lavender and eau-de-Cologne. Between one dish and the next, since the dinner was completely based on tactile pleasures, the guests were to let their fingertips feast uninterruptedly on their neighbour's pyjamas.

In the introduction to her translation of *La Cucina Futuristica* Lesley Chamberlain describes Marinetti's poetic mentors as including the French poets Baudelaire and Rimbaud, both of whom suggested a mixing of sensation in their poetic works. The mixing of sensation is a theme that has a great deal of influence at the turn of the twentieth century and this will be considered again in Chapter 5.

Marinetti's intention is to stimulate directly all five senses simultaneously as a means of mixing sensation. But what would he make of the case of an individual who claims no need of such a contrivance, as for him taste would naturally be accompanied by a tactile sensation? Just such a case has been reported by an American neurologist, Richard Cytowic, in his recent book *The Man Who Tasted Shapes (TMWTS)*. In the opening chapter Richard describes an event at which Michael, his host, upon tasting the chicken sauce, announces 'there aren't enough points on the chicken'. Richard deals with this unusual statement in a kindly fashion and concludes Chapter 1 of *TMWTS* by explaining to Michael that he has synaesthesia.

Warm and sweet, or cool and sour?

It is worth mentioning at this point that the walls between our senses are not as solid as we generally believe. A recent paper in the journal *Nature* provides a fascinating account of how two researchers managed to induce the sensation of taste simply by changing the temperature of small areas of the tongue. For some participants in their study, warming the front of the tongue to temperatures between 20 and 35 °C created a mild but clear sweet sensation. Cooling the same area resulted in the perception of a sour or salty taste. These are ordinary experimental participants having taste sensations induced by temperature change, but this is clearly qualitatively different from the account of Michael's synaesthesia given by Dr Cytowic. As befits all qualitative differences, it has a special term, 'synaesthesia'.

The Greeks have a word for it

So, a definition, what is synaesthesia, or, in the US, synesthesia? The word is a blend of the Greek words for 'sensation' (*aisthesis*) and 'together', or 'union' (*syn*), implying the experience of two, or more, sensations occurring together. It is worth pointing out at this juncture that, in our experience of meeting and testing people with synaesthesia, in almost all cases it is a visual sensation caused by auditory stimulation. This observation is broadly consistent with the historical literature, as reflected in the use of another popular term for the condition of *Audition Colourée* (French for coloured hearing) and *Farbenheren* (the German term). However, as is apparent from Richard Cytowic's descriptions, other forms of the condition have been reported. Much of this book will describe our experience of studying individuals with coloured hearing. However, as our philosophy has always been to challenge our beliefs about the condition, we have studied, often in great detail, individuals who claim to have other forms of synaesthesia.

Consequently, accounts of these other variants of the condition are included. What will also become clear during the course of this book is that the word synaesthesia is a very broad term that is used to describe a variety of events and behaviours. The synaesthesia that Simon Baron-Cohen and I have investigated with the assistance of others is a very specific form with a narrow definition. I have chosen to label this form 'idiopathic synaesthesia' to differentiate it from the other forms that will be discussed in this book.

Science and the burden of proof

As mentioned in the Preface, as well as being an account of scientific investigations into synaesthesia, there are two other motives for writing this book. First, to share with the reader those things I have found interesting and wished I'd known about earlier. Clearly, I can only guess at what you, the current reader, knows. Nevertheless, I ardently hope that at least once in the book you will comment to yourself 'That's interesting, I didn't know about it'. Second, to give those readers unfamiliar with scientific method a helpful introduction to the assumptions, advantages, flaws and pitfalls of neuroscience.

This second motive, to inform the reader about the scientific endeavour and an account of the rules that govern science, causes me some mild concern. There is a danger that this book, designed to be a light read, may become overly pedagogic. I've therefore tried to break up the scientific method sections into digestible pieces. To begin with, it is important to share my personal prejudices with you, as it may well be that we do not hold the same basic views concerning 'the nature of things'. Experience of lecturing on synaesthesia to a wide variety of audiences has taught me that this initial 'chat' will at least make you aware of the assumptions that I make in my scientific work, as well as perhaps cause you to wonder how on earth someone could hold such a view.

The confessions of a physicalist

As mentioned in the Preface, this book has been structured on the kind of lecture I have been asked to give in recent years. Often these lectures have been given either to interested members of the public or to those with an interest in art, literature or cinematography and sometimes even scientists. Having the opportunity to present to such diverse groups of individuals has made me acutely aware that many non-scientists view the psychological universe in a very different way to most, but not all, scientists. Essentially the issue is to do with how many kinds of psychological 'stuff' might exist and to begin with I'd like to examine this issue and declare my own prejudices.

Physical, spiritual and mental stuff

The Latin word for 'reader' is 'lector'. You may have known this before reading it but, for the purposes of this discussion, let us assume you've just discovered this fact and are now intrigued that Thomas Harris should have christened everybody's favourite serial killer with the name Hannibal 'reader'. If you can now recall this fact then there has been an addition to your memory. In everyday parlance this is described as a mental event; your mental life has been enhanced with new information. Take a moment to contemplate this and now ask yourself where that contemplation is occurring? Your first thought might have been that thought happens in a mental 'stuff', but perhaps you imagined that thoughts also happen in the tissue that makes up our central nervous system? The standard view of neuroscience is that your brain has physically changed to accommodate this new fact. We're not sure how this happens

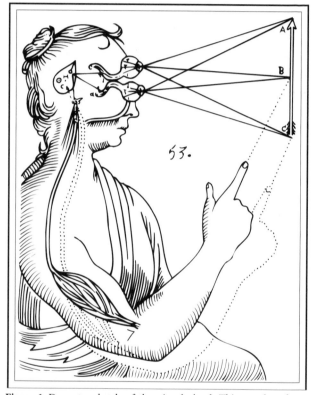

Figure 1 Descartes sketch of the pineal gland. This woodcut from Descartes' 1644 *Principles of Philosophy* illustrates Descartes' theory of vision and its interaction with the pineal gland. Descartes believed that light rays impressed subtle particles into the eyes. The image was then transmitted to the pineal gland, which served as the connection between mind and body. In this sketch the external stimulus is translated into an act of will, in this case 'pointing' by the pineal gland.

exactly, but we are sure that something physical has happened. But what is the relationship between the two events? One view is that there are two kinds of stuff, the mental stuff, in which the thought exists, and physical stuff which is where the memory is stored. This was the view held by the influential French philosopher Rene Descartes (1596–1650) who suggested that the universe is made up of the physical world (*res extensor*) and the mental world (*res cognitans*). Unfortunately, positing the existence of two kinds of 'stuff' leaves an unresolved issue – how do the two types of stuff influence one another? This is a good question. Descartes unpersuasively suggested that the pineal gland (Figure 1) is the point at which the two interact.

Another commentator, Nobel prize-winning physiologist Sir John Eccles (1903–1997), has suggested that the interaction between the physical and the mental may happen at the quantum level. He may be right.

A further possibility is that adopted by most neuroscientists, who assume that, when talking about the mental and the physical, we are simply using two different vocabularies to describe what is fundamentally the same thing. With this model it is possible to explain all events using the vocabulary of different branches of science, a relationship shown in Figure 2.

According to this hierarchical view it should be possible to explain any psychological phenomena using the vocabulary of, in descending order, psychology, physiology, anatomy, biology, biochemistry and physics.

So who is right? Well, we don't know, though opinions are strongly held, and it is vital to remember that all views are intellectually respectable perspectives. Let's also add the possibility of spiritual life for consideration – is this a portion of mental life, or qualitatively different again and

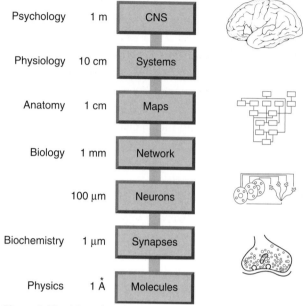

Figure 2 The hierarchy of neuroscience. This figure illustrates a theoretical hierarchy of the some of the disciplines involved in neuro-scientific research, together with an indication of the level at which the discipline tends to operate. Not too much should be read into psychology's position at the top of the hierarchy. Reprinted with permission from Churchland PS and Sejnowski TJ (1988). Perspectives on cognitive neuroscience. *Science*, **242**: 741–5. American Association for the Advancement of Science.

therefore a third kind of stuff? What is abundantly clear to me is that I don't know and that a full discussion is beyond the remit of this book. However, lest we scientists get too cosy, it is worth pointing out that not even physicalists necessarily agree with one another.

So let me declare my prejudices. I am strictly a physicalist; namely, in my world there is only one kind of stuff, the physical stuff. Worse than that, I also believe that if some psychological concepts prove to be hard to find at other levels of science, we should then seriously consider offloading them – thus I probably qualify as an adherent of eliminative physicalism. That some of the psychological concepts we currently believe to exist may well turn out to be epiphenomenal I take to be axiomatic. However, I am unable to adduce any categorical evidence in support of my assumption and so I also allow for the possibility that I might well be entirely wrong.

Welcome to the BBC

As you can see from the hierarchy of science diagram, it would be possible to explain synaesthesia in a number of ways. Some psychologists (the Behaviourists, more on whom in Chapter 2) restrict themselves to speaking about observable behaviour. Others use reference terms from both behaviour and cognition. Yet others allow themselves to speak about the biological basis of behaviour, the 'brain'. For the purposes of this book I will allow myself the luxury of referring to brain, behaviour and cognition or, as I will refer to it, 'the BBC'. However, before continuing let us consider this tripos in a little more detail. Figure 3 should help to make the relationship clearer.

An explanation of any human act could be couched at any level of the BBC. To illustrate this, let us consider the 'lector' reference cited above. If you were here in front of me now I could ask you 'What does "lector" mean in English?' and you would hopefully reply 'reader'. My noting your response would be my evaluation of your behaviour and, on the basis of my observing your behaviour, I would conclude that the recollection of that fact provided me with evidence that you now had a memory trace for it. Finally,

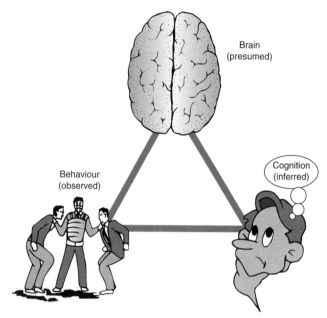

Figure 3 Brain, behaviour, and cognition. The basic assumption made in neuroscience is that our behaviour is controlled by our brain. We therefore work on the presumption that observable behaviour is correlated with certain events taking place within the brain. However, we do not understand the workings of the brain sufficiently to describe functionally what is taking place. We instead have an every-day vocabulary of terms, such as 'thinking', 'memory', 'concentration', 'learning', 'attention', etc. that we can use to describe the brain events. These mental processes are collectively referred to as cognition. Because they are unobservable, but resonate with our intuitions, we infer their existence.

because I am a physicalist I would assume that, for you to remember this fact, some physical change had taken place in your brain. Clearly the behaviour is measurable; I can check to see if you did in fact know the correct translation of lector. The brain bit is a little more difficult, though techniques that allow me to detect changes in your brain when you learn something new are emerging. However, the cognition can only be inferred; the object or process known as memory is something that we assume must exist.

The story with synaesthesia follows a similar line. I can measure a synaesthete's ability to describe accurately their colour experience for specific sounds. Using brain imaging techniques (see Chapter 6) I can also show that the brain activity of a synaesthete during their synaesthetic experience is different to that of a non-synaesthete. What I cannot 'see' is the cognition that links the brain to the behaviour. Nevertheless, a complete account of synaesthesia requires an explanation couched at each level of the BBC hierarchy. In our edited book on synaesthesia, Simon Baron-Cohen and I outlined a theory designed to explain the condition by linking different levels of the hierarchy. In the following section I shall reiterate this theory. There have been, as one might expect, a number of theories put forward to explain synaesthesia and, in later chapters, I will describe and discuss those of which I am aware. However, let us begin with our current view.

Starting with the conclusion

Scientific accounts, when written in a narrative style, usually present a variety of intellectual canapés, an appetizer and then a main course, finally treating the reader to a dessert containing an explanation of the topic under scrutiny. Unconventionally, I have chosen to present you with dessert at the beginning of the book.

Forewarned is forearmed. . .

In an experiment into memory conducted by Bransford & Johnson in 1972, one group of participants was presented with the following prose:

> The procedure is actually quite simple. First you arrange items into different groups. Of course one pile may be sufficient depending on how much there is to do. If you have to go somewhere else due to lack of facilities that is the next step; otherwise, you are pretty well set. It is important not to overdo things. That is, it is better to do too few things at once rather than too many. In the short run this may not seem important but complications can easily arise. A mistake can be expensive as well. At first, the whole procedure will seem complicated. Soon, however, it will become just another facet of life. It is difficult to foresee any end to the necessity of this task in the immediate future, but then, one never can tell. After the procedure is completed one arranges the materials into their appropriate places. Eventually, they will be used once more and the whole cycle will then have to be repeated.

If you consider this passage to be incomprehensible, you are in good company – so too did the participants alluded to above. However, if, at the outset, I had told you that the title of this piece was 'washing clothes' you might have made more sense of the text. Participants in the experiment who were given the title reported finding the passage easy to understand and recalled more of the passage than the first group.

A similar effect might hold true for this book in that, if I describe here our theory of the cause of synaesthesia, it might be easier for you, the reader, to see the relevance and importance of the work described in the following chapters.

A theory of synaesthesia

A number of theories have been posited to account for the condition. These will be reviewed in Chapter 8, but for now there follows the theory that Simon Baron-Cohen and I outlined in Chapter 7 of our book *Synaesthesia: Classic and Contemporary Readings*, which we would, of course, heartily recommend to the interested reader.

It is popularly held by psychologists that we all suffer infantile amnesia; that is to say, we rarely have any recollection of events prior to approximately 3–4 years of age. Some of you, the readers, are already taking issue, and indeed a number of individuals of my acquaintance are adamant that they can recollect events from their early childhood. Of course it might be that the events these individuals can recollect are 'memories' they have unwittingly reconstructed on hearing third parties relate the events. There is considerable evidence to suggest that our memories are not 'veridical', i.e. a perfect film-like recollection, but reconstructive, i.e. a construction of what happened, or what we thought happened. In our research, when we ask people how long they have had synaesthesia, they typically say 'as long as I can remember' and we record at least from 3 to 4 years. It is, of course, entirely possible that people we test and confirm as synaesthetes have had the condition from birth and perhaps even before then. I mention this simply because our theory holds that we are, all of us, synaesthetes for the first 2–3 months of our lives, a time that we are later unable to recall.

As already mentioned, I have taken the hierarchy of science model as my guide. In the next section our theory is described and the explanation couched using the vocabularies of the disciplines listed in Figure 2.

The anatomical level of explanation

As we shall see in Chapter 3, the human brain seems to be organized into a number of specialist areas. Extensive study of the occipital lobes (at the rear, or posterior of the head) confirms that it is in this region that visual information received by the eye is processed. We also know that information received by the ear (auditory data) is, for the most part, processed in regions of the temporal lobe. It is popularly held that no brain cell is more than seven times removed from any other, so clearly all cells are in some sense connected. However, as we do not tend to confuse visual and auditory data, it seems reasonable to suppose that there is sufficient difference between these two functionally specialized brain regions. This is generally the case for adults, but what about children?

There appears to be some functional specialization in neonates, though this might be restricted to basic visual processing. The reason for this assertion is that neonates are capable of making gross visual discrimination. It is also often pointed out that brain cells (neurons) in the primary visual cortex are relatively well insulated from one another from birth, in contrast to other brain areas. As the information transmitted by neurons is electrochemical in nature, it is clearly important that the electrical 'spark' that conveys information does not leak into neighbouring neurons. To prevent this, neurons develop coats of a fatty tissue that effectively insulates one neuron from another. This fatty tissue, known as myelin, grows around the neuron in concentric layers. It would appear that some brain regions do not become effectively myelinated until adolescence and early adulthood. This is a feature of prefrontal lobe development, the brain region believed by many to be the seat of so-called 'higher cognitive functioning' such as planning, abstract reasoning and the control of behaviour. Thus the impetuousness of youth may be due to little more than a lack of fat around your brain cells.

The physiological level of explanation

Our understanding of the functional anatomy of the brain has revealed that the areas that receive and process auditory information are distinct from those areas receiving visual information. For most of us the activity of these areas would appear to be successfully insulated so that audition doesn't intrude on vision, but perhaps for synaesthetes this is either not or less the case? I may be accused of leading with my chin here, but we currently have no direct evidence that synaesthetes have an active pathway between auditory and visual centres. This is, of course, largely because the kind of experiments we would need to do to find this empirical support are unethical. Consequently we need to draw upon what is often called 'convergent' evidence for the plausibility of our theory. Fortunately useful convergent evidence exists and this will be reviewed in the next section.

Some time ago Dr Daphne Maurer of the McMaster University in Toronto drew to our attention some useful facts about the response to sensory stimulation in a number of species. There is, it seems, substantial evidence for the existence of direct connections between auditory and visual areas in the macaque monkey and the cat. However, one small caveat should be attached; it seems that these pathways are short-lived, typically disappearing about 3 months into postnatal development. There is no evidence for the existence of such connections in humans, but as nature tends to hang onto an idea, it seems reasonable to suppose that we go through a similar stage of development. In fact, there is some indirect evidence for a similar stage in our species, details of which will be discussed shortly.

Assuming that similar, transient projections may also be found in humans, what implications might this have? The first, and perhaps most profound, is that, on this evidence, it seems likely that we all of us have synaesthesia until about 3 months of age. So, what is the evidence in support of this notion?

Booming, buzzing confusion?

A debate that pervades virtually the whole of psychology is that concerning the relative importance of genetic make-up (nature) and of experience (nurture). This nature–nurture debate has been a topic of considerable discussion in the consideration of how well equipped the newborn is to make sense of his or her world. Two schools of thought have debated this; the empiricists, whose tradition can be traced back to the writing of the philosopher John Locke, and the 'nativists'. Locke contended that when we are born our mind is a *Tabula rasa* (blank slate) upon which experience can write. Nativists tend to take the view that human neonates are in fact well prepared to make sense of their world from birth. Contemporary psychology tends to take a middle view, supposing that both nature and nurture play crucial roles. It is clear that neonates do seem to be attracted to certain stimulus configurations, especially faces, though it is also true that experience tends to shape the way in which they perceive the world. How do we know this? After all, you cannot ask neonates the kind of questions one could ask of an older participant. Fortunately, developmental psychologists have become very adept at designing elegant experiments in which evidence of specific responses and behaviours is collected with which to infer cognitive activity. One method is to make direct measurements of electrical brain activity and before further considering the neonatal response to stimulation, let us look at some of the techniques neuroscience uses to measure the electrical activity of the brain.

EEGs and evoked potentials

A traditional method for examining the electrical activity of the brain is the technique of electroencephalography, or

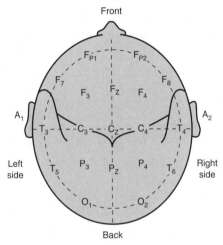

Figure 4 Standard electrode placement sites for electroencephalography (EEG). The 10–20 lead system is based on the relationship between the location of an electrode and the underlying area of cerebral cortex. Each point on this figure indicates a possible electrode position. Each site has a letter (to identify the lobe) and a number or another letter to identify the hemisphere location. The letters F, T, C, P, and O stand for frontal, temporal, central, parietal, and occipital, respectively. (Note that there is no 'central lobe'; this is used for identification purposes.) Even numbers (2, 4, 6, 8) refer to the right hemisphere and odd numbers (1, 3, 5, 7) refer to the left hemisphere. The z refers to an electrode placed on the midline. Also note that the smaller the number, the closer the position is to the midline.

EEG for short. This technique was first used by a Liverpudlian physician, Richard Caton (1842–1926), to record changes in brain activity that accompany movement in animal subjects. Caton originally measured activity directly from the surface of the brain, but later discovered that signals could be obtained by recording from the skull. EEG has in recent years become more accurate at detecting where in the brain electrical changes are occurring and has proven to be of particular clinical use in the monitoring and detection of epilepsy, a neurological condition character- ized by the presence of abnormal electrical discharges in the brain (Figure 4).

One of Caton's most dramatic demonstrations of the technique was to show marked increases in electrical activity when a light shone in the eyes of the participant. This was perhaps the earliest demonstration of a paradigm that has come to be known as evoked potentials. This shows that it is possible to stimulate specific sensory sys- tems and detect activity in areas of the brain known to deal with this information. So, for example, if one looks for visually evoked potentials (VEPs), then typically changes in the activity of the visual cortex are observed. Similarly, auditorily evoked potentials (AEPs) typically yield changes in electrical signals from the temporal lobes. These pat- terns of stimulation and electrical activity correlations are seen in normal adult participants and in young children, but not in neonates, at least not before about 3 months of age. Instead, and remarkably, when an auditory event is presented to a neonate, a signal is observed to come from visual areas in the occipital cortex. Dr Maurer has also reported interesting effects in studies of somatosensory evoked potentials (SEPs). Normally the amplitude of SEPs increases as a consequence of tactile stimulation. However, it has been observed that neonates show increases in the response of their SEPs when played white noise, an auditory event.

So, there is no direct evidence, but plenty of indirect evidence, for early transitory pathways that carry auditory information to visual areas of the brain. The theory then, holds that these pathways are preserved into adulthood in people with synaesthesia, whereas the rest of us lose this ability somewhere around 3 months of age when changes in the structure and connectivity of the brain allow us to differentiate between input from the different senses. A positive aspect for the acceptance of this theory is that rather than have to posit the growth of a 'new', supranormal connection in synaesthetes, we can instead countenance the possibility that a pathway is left intact after the usual period. An interesting possibility then, is that we were, all of us, synaesthetes for a time. For some commentators on synaesthesia this is just as expected. Take, for example, the French existentialist philosopher Maurice Merleau-Ponty (1908–1961) who, writing in 1945, stated that in his view:

> Synaesthetic perception is the rule, and we are unaware of it only because scientific knowledge shifts the centre of gravity of experience, so that we unlearn how to see, hear, and generally speaking, feel.

An interesting perspective on the issue, but we scientists don't have the luxury of simply asserting the importance of the primacy of perception; we have to come up with a little more in the way of evidence. Meanwhile, back with our theory. It is all fine and dandy to muster up the notion that auditory information finds its way to visual areas via perpetuated neonatal pathways, but what leads to these pathways being maintained? Some possible mechanisms are considered in the next section.

The molecular biological level of explanation

So, the physiological and anatomical accounts hang together, but how do visual and auditory areas get connected in the first place? And, if the theory is correct, why is this connection only maintained in some individuals? A sad fact of life is that once your early brain development has concluded, you cannot grow any more neurons. Even more distressing is the loss of several hundred neurons per day in the average adult. Fortunately, we have quite a lot to start with; in the normal brain many more than we need, i.e. we have a lot of spare or 'redundant' brain cells. For example, Parkinson's disease seems to be caused by damage to a discrete area of the brain, the substantia nigra, literally the black mass, so-called because of the melanin contained in this brain region. However, it seems that it is only once about 80% of the brain cells in this region are lost that the cardinal signs of tremor, rigidity, slowness of movement (bradykinesia) and unstable posture become apparent. It seems that, because of our progressive brain cell loss, we need considerable redundancy to function normally. You will doubtless have heard the assertion that we use only about 10% of our brain, the logic being that if only we could activate the rest of this apparently idle tissue we would all instantly become fabulously intelligent? This optimistic view presupposes that it is possible to activate this tissue. A second, perhaps less romantic view, is that all that tissue is there because we need a lot to start with, so that we can still function successfully once a lifetime of brain cell loss has occurred.

However, substantial brain cell death occurs early in life. In fact it is a particularly early event, occurring in the first few months of life. This seems paradoxical: why have so much brain cell production during fetal development just to have huge numbers of cells self-destruct during the first year of life? Current thinking is that this event is also related to redundancy, only this time cell death is best regarded as judicious pruning. It would seem that perinatal brain cell death occurs so that individual brains can be as well shaped as possible for surviving in the environment in which the individual finds him or herself. The presumption is that this process (apoptosis) is determined according to the individual's experience as well as his or her genetic make-up. Presumably this process of slimming down the brain yields a more efficient organ, 'shaped' by experience and genetic predisposition to be as well suited to its environment as possible. So how does this process impact on our understanding of the mechanisms of synaesthesia?

The explanation couched at the anatomical level posits that there are discrete neuroanatomical structures responsible for processing auditory and visual information. The physiological explanation connects these two centres and provides a pathway by which incoming neural stimulation can stimulate visual areas. But why should this happen in so small a group of individuals? As will be seen in Chapter 7, there is some evidence to suggest that synaesthesia may be an inherited condition. If this is the case then the presence of synaesthesia might indicate that neonatal pathways between auditory and visual areas are maintained in those genetically predisposed to have synaesthesia. So, for example, in non-synaesthetes the process of apoptosis may cause the early auditory to visual area pathways to be pruned. In those genetically programmed for synaesthesia these pathways may be maintained. One pleasing aspect to this theory is the lack of need for an additional pathway, a supranormal connection between audition and vision. This is still, of course, a possibility, but parsimony suggests that a preserved, early pathway is a more satisfying proposition than an extraordinary connection in the synaesthetic brain.

Finally, a psychological theory. . .

The account so far has sought to explain synaesthesia using the vocabularies of physical sciences such as anatomy, physiology, and molecular biochemistry. But what are the consequences of this hypothesized connecting pathway for the synaesthetes' experience of the condition? One way to view this is to borrow the notion of modularity from anatomy and try to couch our psychological explanation in modular terms. For us to 'know' that a percept is visual, auditory, olfactory, etc. we must have developed a method of identifying information as being of one sensory kind or another. There is therefore likely to be a modular structure to sensation that allows for discrete identification of information as being specific to a sensory system. Modularity is an oft-found assumption in psychology, though is by no means without its critics. This concept is discussed in a little more detail again in Chapter 3, but for now it is sufficient to say that our modularity theory holds that, whereas in non-synaesthetes audition and vision are functionally discrete, in individuals with synaesthesia a breakdown in modularity has occurred. The consequence of this, in the case of coloured hearing synaesthesia, is that sounds have visual attributes.

How could we prove the theory?

One method of investigation would be to look at the brains of people with synaesthesia to establish whether such pathways are present. Neuroimaging techniques of the sort discussed in Chapter 6 are sadly not yet sensitive enough to detect such pathways, though recent developments using diffusion and perfusion-weighted imaging hold considerable promise. One other method of identifying abnormal brain configurations is to examine the brain at post mortem. So, for example, if the brain can be obtained sufficiently soon after its owner has expired, even the neurochemical state can be accurately determined. Differences in gross anatomy and cell number and structure can also be quite readily characterized, but tracing pathways after death is still too much of a challenge. Some progress has been made in developing tracer chemicals that can be used postmortem, but not in myelinated tissue such as is found in the adult brain. It seems that we must wait for further advances in the technical repertoire of neuroanatomists and physiologists.

The last hundred years have thrown up a number of proposed explanations of synaesthesia and some of these will be discussed later in the book. However, the stage is now set for an exploration of what is known about synaesthesia and those that have the condition.

CHAPTER 2

Renaissance

I am writing this chapter just a few days after the end of the last millennium. As we might have expected, the arbitrary change from 1999 to 2000 was not accompanied by planes falling from the sky, civil disorder, or the gradual unfolding of the apocalyptic Revelations of St John. Nevertheless, the end of the last century was accompanied by much anxiety, pontification, and hyperbolic accounts of imminent disaster. What's fascinating about *fin de siècle* fever, as we might call it, is that the issues of major concern in 1899 and 1999 appear to be very similar. A favourite book of mine, *France fin de siècle*, by Eugen Weber, contains descriptions of the concerns of the day that uncannily mirror our own. Concern about the creation of an underclass, the relentless pace of technology, and escalating crime all feature and are quoted in terms that make the rhetoric and hyperbole of the modern day tabloid press seem quite tame. For example, in the healthcare industry there was concern about 'a nervous weakness to which young adults appeared particularly prone and which manifested itself in physical and mental lassitude, listlessness, lack of energy and enthusiasm, and a general sense of weariness', a disease labelled 'neurasthenia' but sounding for all the world like ME ('Yuppie flu') to the modern ear.

Of particular interest to the student of synaesthesia is that there was a strong interest in the condition at about this time. In fact, many of the observations to be found in the contemporary literature are mirrored in the literature that accumulated between 1880 and 1920. Also, a curiosity of the last hundred years of study is a period of about fifty years during which virtually no work on the condition appears to have been published. In this chapter I shall seek to draw some parallels between modern day work on the condition and that carried out at the end of the last century, as well as to explain the fifty-year silence. As there has been a renaissance of interest in synaesthesia in recent years, I shall permit myself the luxury of referring to the late nineteenth-century literature as the 'classical' literature and the modern day equivalent as the 'contemporary' literature.

The mists of time...

One of the most useful pieces of research on the topic of synaesthesia was a research article published in the *Psychological Bulletin* by Lawrence Marks. A particularly useful component of Professor Marks' account was his summary of published work on the topic of visual auditory synaesthesia, references to which he traces back as far as Pythagoras in the sixth century BC. From a psychologist's point of view this chronology has several fascinating characteristics, but two that are particularly noteworthy. The first deals with the relative flood of publications on synaesthesia that occurred in the 1880s and 1890s. These dates coincide with the founding of Wilhelm Wundt's laboratory in Leipzig (in 1889), which, as students of the history of psychology will know, is the point at which the discipline of psychology is generally acknowledged to have been born. It is also interesting that the first wave of research into psychology should have featured the study of synaesthesia, with no less than 27 published articles appearing in the period between 1882 and 1892 (Figure 5), but it is odd

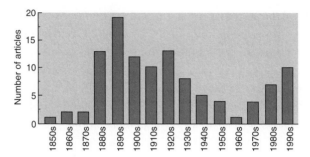

Figure 5 Published papers on synaesthesia from the 1850s to the 1990s. This bar chart shows the number of papers published in each decade over a 140-year period. As you can see, there was considerable interest in the 1880s and 1890s, with a marked tailing off during the years in which behaviourism held sway as the dominant psychological paradigm. Interest has increased steadily since a low point in the 1960s.

that this flood should have so quickly turned to a trickle.

In common with most psychological studies of the time, these reports were almost exclusively simple descriptive accounts of single cases, or series, of individuals with synaesthesia. Scientists of the day would scrupulously collect data and report it using averages and measures of the distribution of the data, so-called 'descriptive statistics'. However, science requires a method of deciding whether results are likely to be due to simple chance variation or because of a real phenomenon. Scientists working at the close of the nineteenth century did not have access to these inferential statistical methods and therefore no way of testing the veracity of their theories. Nevertheless, many of the theories and experimental findings of the late nineteenth century have been reinvestigated by modern day scientists and found to be essentially correct. In later chapters, especially in Chapter 6, dealing with brain imaging, we'll have the chance to consider how a contemporary technological breakthrough can further our understanding of synaesthesia. To set the ground for the coverage of contemporary literature, in the following section I'll review the main findings of the classical literature and describe some of the key studies published between 1880 and 1920, beginning with the account given by Sir Francis Galton in his book *Inquiries into Human Faculty*, published in 1883.

A eugenecist speaks

Sadly Sir Francis will be likely to be remembered for his well-intentioned but repugnant views on how we should maintain the nobility of our species by controlling breeding, extending as far as compulsory sterilization of those regarded as inferior. Less well known is his chapter on synaesthesia, an account that details the synaesthetic experiences of several individuals of Galton's acquaintance. Whilst we cannot be sure that these individuals would pass the stringent criteria applied to most contemporary scientific studies of synaesthesia, there are a number of details that are strikingly similar to the results of our work. An excellent example is Galton's closing account of the specificity of his participants' accounts of their synaesthesic perceptions:

> Persons who have colour associations are unsparingly
> critical. To ordinary individuals one of these accounts
> seems just as wild and lunatic as another, but when one seer
> is submitted to another seer, who is sure to see the colours
> in a different way, the latter is scandalised and almost angry
> at the heresy of the former.

Anyone who has been in a room with two synaesthetes will recognize the scene that Galton describes. One of the most remarkable experiences we have had during the decade in which we have studied synaesthesia was the inaugural meeting of the International Synaesthesia Association at Charing Cross & Westminster Medical School in 1995. Imagine a whole medical school conference area of synaesthetes comparing notes on their colour associations. The fact that synaesthetes argue and seldom, if ever, agree what colour each word should be is also scientifically interesting, and something we will revisit later in this chapter.

The classical literature

Our experience of the last ten years has yielded a variety of interesting cases of synaesthesia. For the most part, our investigations have been limited to instances of coloured hearing synaesthesia. This is because we have tried to ensure that we are dealing with a homogeneous group of participants. With every additional piece of media coverage we have enlarged the number of synaesthetes who have discovered our activities. Inevitably this collection has thrown up instances of synaesthetes who do not fit the criteria for our usual studies. We have, when time has allowed, studied these individuals (for more on this see Chapter 6). In many cases there are similar examples in the classical literature, providing a neat link between the work of scientists a hundred years ago and contemporary efforts to understand and explain the condition. The contemporary work on these issues will be discussed in later chapters, but here is a sample of what I regard to be the most germane research monographs printed between 1880 and 1920.

Note on colour hearing – the case of GL

'In 1887 I met a remarkable case of color-hearing'. So begins Professor Frederick Starr's account of a series of three assessments of the same individual, GL, 'a young lady of unusually quick and bright mind, she has some artistic power and is a writer of ability'. In his account of GL a number of themes and comments familiar to contemporary research on synaesthesia emerge. For example, GL was apparently aware of her synaesthesia from early childhood. She also related that, as a very little girl, she was laughed at because she said that names were coloured. Both these themes emerged during interviews with contemporary synaesthetes, as I shall discuss later in the book (see Chapter 4). Starr was aware that synaesthetic percepts were constant across time and had an excellent opportunity to show empirically that GL was capable of reproducing identical colour descriptions on each of the three occasions on which she was tested (1887, 1891, and 1893). Unfortunately, different lists were used on each occasion and so this chance was missed. However, from a later report made in the journal *Nature* it seems that a Professor Holden, on discovering that his daughter Mildred had colour associations, conducted just such a study. Professor Holden constructed a list composed of numbers, letters, days of the week, etc., first noting down Mildred's colour associations when she was 8 years old. Mildred was subsequently retested at the ages of $10\frac{1}{2}$, 13, $14\frac{1}{2}$, and $17\frac{1}{2}$ years. It seems that on each occasion she perfectly reproduced the same colours, leading William O. Krohn to comment in 1893 that 'The agreement of these different lists is most remarkable, showing very plainly that it is not a case of mere memory, but one of vivid and permanent association'.

Starr concludes his 1893 article with some notes on synaesthesia in the blind. He notes that amongst the congenitally blind there was no concept of colour 'and no tendency to imagine it in terms of other sensations'. This seems reasonable, but at odds with a reference often cited in pieces on synaesthesia concerning a blind man and his conception of the colour scarlet. The quote comes to us from a creditable source, the philosopher John Locke (1632–1704):

> A studious blind man who had mightily beat his head about a visible object, and made use of the explications of his books and friends, to understand those names of light and colours, which often came his way, betrayed one day that he now understood what scarlet signified. Upon which, his friend demanded what scarlet was? The blind man answered, it was like the sound of a trumpet.

Although this is often cited, it requires an awfully big leap of faith to suppose that this genuinely represents an early account of synaesthesia. What is most interesting from Starr's comments is his suspicion that 'those who become blind in childhood, after learning colours, very soon come to perceive colour sensations in their hearing'. Starr based this supposition on his finding that three of six individuals who fulfilled this criterion appeared to have 'colour hearing to a marked degree'. In contrast, six individuals either born blind or who were blind since infancy had no synaesthetic experience. Starr concludes his report by suggesting that 'The colour-sound and mental imagery of the blind is, I am convinced, an interesting special field of study'. Recent research suggests he may have been right. We'll revisit this theme in the final chapter of the book.

A case of synaesthesia (1914)

Charles Myers had the good fortune to meet Alexander Scriabin, one of the historical figures most often described as a synaesthete. In fact, there is considerable doubt about the legitimacy of Scriabin's claim, or rather the claims made on his behalf, as we shall discuss in Chapter 5. The year before Myers reported an account of his meeting with Scriabin he described the case of a 30 year old man who claimed to see colours in response to hearing single tones and chords. Much of Myers' account is a description of the colours elicited by tones delivered via a tuning fork or other devices such as 'a Galton whistle' or an 'Appun's Tonmesser'. Of particular interest are the general descriptions and circumstances surrounding the synaesthesia which, as we shall see, were also reported by the synaesthetes we interviewed and which will be described in later chapters. Myers' participant A, for example, reports having had synaesthesia for as long as he can remember. Of particular interest are the subjective accounts of the synaesthetic experience. A clearly states 'I don't *see* the colours in my mind, I have no imagery of them'. He is equally clear that the visual presentation of sheets of a separate colour does not impact on his synaesthetic experience. Myers comments that A's synaesthesia is 'exceedingly rare', a reference to the fact that his synaesthesia is restricted to sounds, but not words. Myers' observation meshes with our own experience, in that the majority of synaesthetes we have encountered are instances of synaesthesia for groups of words, typically days of the week, months, seasons, and numbers. More on this later. Myers also prefigures our own notions regarding the causes of synaesthesia. For example, he comments that synaesthesiae 'may perhaps be ascribed to the persistence of a primitive stage in the differentiation and elaboration of sensations and in the development of their functional inter-relation'.

A case of coloured gustation

As already discussed, cases of anything other than coloured hearing synaesthesia appear to be quite rare and so interest is always piqued by cases such as this one, reported in 1911 by June Downey of the University of Wyoming. She comments at the beginning of her article that cases of coloured taste have been less well described in the literature, though attributes this not to the frequency with which this variant occurs, but to the failure of those with it to notice that tastes (or smells) evoke colours. Downey suggests that this is because objects that smell and/or taste are usually bound to an object that naturally has a colour which masks the synaesthesic colour. This may or may not be true, but it is our experience that those with, say, coloured smell are very aware of the colour of the odiferous object, as well as the colour percept elicited by the smell.

Downey's participant, S, reports having experienced coloured gustation for as long as he can remember. In contrast to our experience with coloured hearing synaesthetes, S was able to locate his synaesthesiae, in this case in the mouth. Intriguingly, S also reported that, whilst some colours were agreeable tastes (such as pink and lavender), others, such as reds and browns, were found to be disagreeable. S never experienced blue tastes. After eliciting these subjective accounts of his synaesthesia, Downey set about answering the following questions:

1. Does S possess a normal sensitivity to taste?

2. Are the colour tones of his tastes uniformly determined by any particular factor in the gustatory complex?

3. Is the induced colour sensational or imaginal?

Downey set out to address these questions by administering these tastes and then recording S's responses. Psychophysical experimentation revealed that S seemed particularly sensitive to small concentrations of saccharin (sweet), salt (sodium chloride), sour (sulphuric acid!), and bitter (quinine). However, S was quite poor at distinguishing some tastes; for example, he was seemingly unable to tell quinine from cayenne pepper and took 3 minutes to identify the taste of peppermint. The answer to question 2 appears to be no, but Downey holds out the hope that 'a thoroughgoing analysis would reveal the existence of a constant and uniform principle which determines the colour tones of various tastes'. On the basis of her findings this hope appears somewhat forlorn as, whilst S was capable of producing simple one colour descriptions for tastes such as quinine (orange–red), the same colour description was also given for red pepper, bitter almonds, and alum. Similarly, saccharin, anise, cherry syrup, sarsaparilla syrup, and tar-water all elicited black. Most curious of all is that, while saccharin evoked a colour percept, granulated and lump sugar yielded no synaesthesiae at all.

Before leaving Downey and her coloured taster, let's consider her third question, regarding whether the synaesthesiae induced were sensational or imaginal. This question will occur repeatedly throughout this book, though in slightly different forms. Essentially the issue is whether simply tasting a substance that elicits colour is both necessary and sufficient to elicit the synaesthesic experience. Put another way, would the synaesthete automatically 'see' the colour on being stimulated with the appropriate odour on each occasion that the odour was presented? If the answer is yes then the perception can be described as sensational, using Downey's parlance. However, if it is necessary for the synaesthete to conjour up the colour in an effortful fashion, then the perception might best be described as imaginal. This distinction is of major importance for our understanding of the various theories and descriptions of synaesthesia. Experience suggests that a definition of terms is helpful in discussing these issues and so I shall propose two different terms to be used to refer to these different scenarios. Where and when I refer to synaesthesiae that are believed to be automatic, constant, and irrepressible I shall use the term 'correspondence' to describe the relationship between the primary sensation and the synaesthesic percept. In contrast, when I am referring to synaesthesiae that are learnt, and therefore not automatic, constant, and irrepressible, I shall use the term 'association'. This may sound like academic pedantry, but the reasons for this clear delineation will become clearer later in the book.

Isador Henry Coriat's (1875–1943) synaesthetes

The year 1913 seems to have brought a variety of synaesthetes to the attention of this Boston doctor. An important caveat to all of these case studies is that in each instance the individual was referred on the basis of having a pre-existing psychiatric disorder. This is not to say that one should necessarily doubt the claims made by such individuals, but it is worth remembering that contemporary neuroscientists often carefully screen experimental participants for psychiatric disorder. This precaution seems sensible, especially when dealing with subjective cognitive states such as synaesthesia. Coriat was probably better known for his work *The Meaning of Dreams* (1915) and for his involvement in psychoanalysis, particularly in Boston where, in 1928, he resurrected the Boston Psychoanalytic Society. Before progressing to a consideration of Coriat's synaesthetes, I'd like to take a slight diversion to clarify commonly found confusion regarding the relationship between psychology, psychiatry, and psychoanalysis. These three very different disciplines are often muddled together, for no better reason than that they all share the same first five letters. For the record, here are definitions for these diverse disciplines.

Psychiatrists are medical doctors who have chosen to specialize in the study of psychiatric disorders such as schizophrenia, bipolar affective disorder, depression, etc.

Psychologists are typically not medically trained and cannot therefore prescribe medication. Many psychologists have counselling and psychotherapy skills.

Psychoanalysts tend, for the most part, to be psychiatrists who have chosen to adopt the philosophies and techniques described by figures in the psychoanalytic (also sometimes called psychodynamic) movement. The best known of these figures is almost certainly Sigmund Freud, though others such as Jung, Klein, and Schilder have also been influential. Thanks for reading, I just wanted to clear that up.

The first of Coriat's accounts is the case of an intelligent 41-year-old woman who had suffered from an anxiety neurosis for a number of years. Coriat, through interview, determined that her synaesthesia predated the onset of her neurosis and the patient confirmed that she had been aware of her synaesthesia since 'the earliest years of childhood'. What remains both remarkable and disappointing about her synaesthesia is that her percepts were restricted in range to various shades of blue. 'Nellie', for example, was a pale, sky blue, whereas 'Lucy' was a clear sapphire. We have never met a synaesthete with so limited a range of the condition. Consistent with our experience of talking to synaesthetes, Coriat's patient confirmed that her synaesthesiae had remained constant; in Coriat's words 'the same sound or word was always associated with the same colour'. A curiosity of this patient's synaesthesia is that the usual trigger words, such as days of the week, numbers, and months of the year, produced no colours. Coriat too supposed that synaesthesia was due to 'a congenital defect of the nervous system, in which the stimulation from one center passes over into another'.

Coriat's second case of the year was a 40-year-old woman who suffered from coloured pain. The lady in question seems to have suffered from a number of problems, including sleepwalking, fatigue (neurasthenic symptoms), and migraine. It was the last of these symptoms that seem to have caused most of her coloured pain, typically a blueness that accompanied severe and persistent headache. Mild headaches tended to elicit white pain synaesthesiae, with deep headaches causing vivid scarlet percepts.

Our final case from Dr Coriat's casebook is not a patient actually seen by him, but a case of synaesthesia presented in abstract form and apparently translated from French by Coriat himself. In fact this synaesthete was seen and tested by a Dr Marinesco, who published his findings in 1912. The subject of this paper was a 35-year-old woman who recounted having had synaesthesia from the age of 6 years. What is remarkable about his case, though familiar to anyone who has ever spoken with a synaesthete about their experiences, is that, until about 14 years of age, the participant 'had not the slightest doubt that everyone experienced a sensation of colour on hearing a spoken word'. Again, this report prefigures our own findings, as we shall see in later chapters.

The Wellesley College project

I shall close this little tour of late nineteenth- and early twentieth-century articles on synaesthesia with a consideration of the broader possibilities for the condition, specifically that it might be rather more commonplace than previous commentators had supposed. Many of the themes I shall address now will also come up for discussion in Chapter 8, where we shall consider the possibility that synaesthesia is, just as Galton suggested, a largely inherited condition.

Many of the articles discussed above point out the relative rarity of synaesthesia. For example, Coriat begins both his accounts with introductions such as 'Cases of synesthesia are sufficiently rare to warrant the recording and analysis of any new observations'. However, a bias is apparent in that none of these studies began with a representative sample of the general population but instead with cases identified through clinical practice or through chance encounter. To estimate accurately how often one finds instances of synaesthesia it is necessary to examine a sample of individuals believed to be representative of the population and find how many have the condition. There will be more on this in Chapter 8, but let us for now examine an early attempt to estimate how frequently synaesthesia is found, the Wellesley College Project.

The study was the brainchild of one Mary Whiton Calkins, at the time an Associate Professor of Psychology at the college. The study was commenced in the spring of 1892, when 525 individuals were queried. At this time a total of 35 people (6.7%) claimed to have what Calkins described as pseudochromasthesia. However, closer examination of the varieties of pseudochromasthesia shows that only four individuals reported having colour percepts for all words, bringing the frequency figure to less than 1%. Professor Calkins echoes Galton when reporting 'to discover exactly the manner in which the colour appears to a subject is very difficult'. Participants questioned about the onset of their synaesthesia again consistently refer to an onset in early childhood, and report near relatives also having the condition.

In addition to providing us with a number of statistical summaries, Professor Calkins also provides detailed case studies of pseudochromasthesia. These case reports are astonishingly similar to those we collected more than a century later and serve to illustrate a number of themes that I will again pick up later in the book. Below are abbreviated accounts of the experiences of two individuals, labelled case A and case B.

Case A

Miss A is a girl about 19 years old, who says that she has had this experience ever since she can remember, but that it has never occurred to her as anything unusual. She sees the colour only when she hears the letter or word; that is, when someone else speaks it. When reading, unless she stops to say the word to herself, she has no impression of colour.

The phenomenon manifests itself with her, especially with letters, both vowels and consonants, and with words, only in so far as the initial letter throws the colour over the rest. For example, as *a* is blue, Alice is blue, and because *s* is yellow, Sunday is yellow.

Case B

Miss B is also about 19 years old. She has had coloured hearing ever since she was a child, long before she could either read or write. With her, however, colours were first associated with names and only later, since she has thought about the matter, has she associated colours with the letters of the alphabet. B's mother first noticed the peculiarity when she was asked to suggest names for the marbles with which the child was playing. The mother proposed names, but B rejected most of them as unsuitable, because, she said, they were not of the same colour as the marbles.

There seems to be no rule governing the association of colours with words. Each separate word and letter has its distinct colour, and if the colours seem to be duplicated there is a decided difference in the shade. For instance, Sarah and Stella, which have the same initial letter, are totally different in colour, the former a bright blue, and the latter a corn colour.

It seems that Professor Calkins continued to monitor successive intakes at Wellesley College and recorded the frequency of pseudochromasthesia. Remarkably, the figure of 6.7% for 1892 more than doubled to 16.82% in 1893 and then rose to 23.3% in 1894. How curious. What could account for such an explosive increase? It seems vanishingly unlikely that synaesthesia became more prevalent, so perhaps interviewees felt an obligation to comply. Perhaps to be one of the 'in-crowd' one had to become a synaesthete? Distinctly possible, one imagines. These odd findings neatly illustrate the dangers of exclusively taking subjective reports of a mental state as prima facie evidence. This is not to say that first person subjective accounts are not important, simply that we need to acquire objective data to support these accounts.

What can we learn from the classical literature?

A number of key findings emerge from the studies discussed above and I have listed them below to serve as an *aide memoire* for later chapters:

- Coloured hearing seems by far the most common form of synaesthesia.

- Other forms, such as coloured taste and coloured pain are reported, but are apparently quite rare.
- Colour word correspondences are highly idiosyncratic.
- Synaesthetes report having had the condition for as long as they can remember.
- Synaesthesiae are not 'seen' with the mind's eye.
- Large sample studies suggest synaesthesia is relatively common.
- Synaesthetes often report family members also having the condition.
- In cases of coloured hearing, merely reading is insufficient to elicit synaesthesiae, the words must be heard.

One final comment, before I move to a discussion of how and why synaesthesia fell from favour. Whilst my review of the classical literature is short of a comprehensive account, it is intriguing how frequently the subjects of these reports are females. The danger with selectively quoting from a literature is that one may accidentally (or sometimes deliberately) convey a false image. However, I recently managed to obtain a copy of an 1893 article from the *American Journal of Psychology* in which the author, William Krohn, comments that, with respect to synaesthesia 'The larger number of the subjects are women'. It is also worth mentioning that he continues in a very unreconstructed way with 'who as a class can hardly be called introspective; at least they are less so than men'. Hmm, a curiosity of nineteenth-century literature perhaps? He offers some comfort to the female sex by ending his sentence with the comment ' – but they are more observant'! As you might imagine, little scientific evidence is mustered in support of these two outrageous generalizations. However, to return to my first point, as long ago as 1893 psychologists had noticed that most synaesthetes are women. This again reveals a link between the classical and contemporary literatures and highlights a theme we shall explore a little later.

Mass extinction

So, widespread interest in synaesthesia coincides with the establishment of psychology as a scientific discipline and features a succession of reports, but little in the way of experimentation. Why? Essentially because experimentation needed a method of determining whether theories of human thinking were true, or not. Such a judgement became possible with the development of probability methods and inferential statistics in the 1920s. But why were these statistical developments so important to scientists? In the next section I'll try to explain.

Why do scientists use statistics?

Essentially scientists use statistics because they want to know whether the results they have obtained in their experiments are due to chance, or due to a 'real' effect. Clearly this needs a little more explanation. As usual, such complex issues are best explained by illustration. I recently came upon an excellent little vignette that neatly shows the role of statistics in experimentation.

Now, what are the chances of that happening?

History has represented the British as a nation of tea drinkers. Evidence for this view is plentiful, but let's take

Marlene Dietrich's view, and slight envy, of the role of tea in the life of the British.

> The British have an umbilical cord which has never been cut and through which tea flows constantly. It is curious to watch them in times of sudden horror, tragedy or disaster. The pulse stops apparently, and nothing can be done, and no move made, until 'a nice cup of tea' is quickly made. There is no question that it brings solace and does steady the mind. What a pity all countries are not so tea-conscious. World-peace conferences would run more smoothly if 'a nice cup of tea' were available at the proper time.

I couldn't have put it better myself. However, how does one make the ideal cup of tea*; more specifically, should one always put the milk in before pouring the tea? A key question here is whether anyone would notice whether the milk had preceded the tea. Such a question exercised the minds of Sir Ronald Aylmer Fisher (1890–1962) and Muriel Bristol. Sir Ronald, a famous statistician, and Miss Bristol (heir to the Wedgwood fortune) were taking tea together when this very question arose. In order to answer it, they conducted a parlour room experiment for which eight cups of tea were prepared. Four of the cups had milk poured into tea, and the other four had tea poured into milk. Sir Ronald (the experimenter) then challenged Miss Bristol to identify correctly which of the eight had the tea added first and which the milk. Miss Bristol correctly identified six of eight brews, an apparently outstanding performance. However, it occurred to Sir Ronald that such an apparently prodigious

---

* For official guidance the reader is invited to consult British Standard BS 6008 (ISO 3103–1980) entitled 'Method for preparation of a liquor of tea for use in sensory tests' which runs to a mere 8 pages.

performance might simply be due to chance. So what are the chances of such a performance? Using Fisher's exact test (you see what eight cups of tea can do for you) we can calculate the probability of Miss Bristol getting six out of eight correct as being 0.243, i.e. approximately one in four. These odds are insufficiently impressive for us to reject the notion that Miss Bristol really could tell the *modus operandi* adopted for the eight cups of tea. This of course begs the question – what odds would we accept as evidence that our results are due to a real effect rather than chance? More on this later.

The mists are clearing

Sir Ronald gave up being a maths teacher in 1919 to take up a position at the Rothamsted Agricultural Experiment Station where he worked as a biologist. However, it was as a statistician that we best remember him, primarily because of his work on small samples (one heiress and eight cups of tea is hardly a large sample) but also his invention of analysis of variance, a statistical technique well known to scientists. Fisher's move to Rothamsted, an agricultural research establishment, appears odd. However, it is as well to bear in mind that the need to compare things like the grain yield of different agricultural techniques required methods for deciding whether one technique was indeed superior to another. This agricultural legacy can still be seen in contemporary statistical nomenclature, as in terms like 'split-plot analysis'.

The rigour of the scientific method used in agriculture, chemistry, biology, etc. provided experimentalists in all areas of science with the opportunity to formulate and test their theories. For psychologists to use this method required that they acquired observable data. Biologists could measure nerve cells, but how does one measure cognition, the thoughts in other people's heads? In the next section we will consider this issue and the solutions proposed by psychologists.

The paradigm shifts

Philosophers and historians of science have noted that the history of science has been punctuated by shifts from one set of assumptions and/or methods to another. The philosophers are also fond of pointing out that these shifts are radical and are usually caused by dissatisfaction with the prevailing paradigm's ability to explain. Probably the most dramatic shift in psychology was the shift from cognitivism to so-called behaviourism that occurred in the 1930s and sounded the death knell for research into synaesthesia for fifty years.

Behaviourism – the nature of the beast

Let's begin with a definition – what exactly does it mean to describe someone as a behaviourist and why did the shift occur? As a result of the developments in inferential statistics that we discussed earlier, science had a defendable method of empirically testing theories that a specified effect was caused by a controlled, prespecified factor. So, in experimental parlance, it was possible to manipulate an independent variable and measure its effect upon a dependent variable. Here is the crux of the dilemma for psychologists interested in cognition – how do you measure it? After all, it is the behaviour that one measures. Take, for example, a simple experiment to test memory in which participants are asked to associate words with colours as best they can in one minute using either mental imagery (mnemonics) or by rote (simple repetition of the words). Typically the experiment will show that participants using mnemonics will remember more words than those using rote. However, the crucial aspect of this experiment is that the cognitive concept of 'memory' is measured by counting the number of words recalled, the participant's 'behaviour'. Thus we are in fact measuring 'number of words recalled' which we take to be a manifestation of memory. A number of influential psychologists in the 1920s and 1930s became concerned about the discipline's reliance upon unobservable hypothetical constructs as a way of explaining behaviour and instead restricted themselves to measuring and reporting what was observable. The learning of a list of words could be described using learning theory, the mainstay of behaviouristic thinking.

Pavlov and his famous salivating dogs

What influenced so many psychologists so dramatically? Interestingly, it appears to have been the work of the Russian physiologist Ivan Pavlov, a man who, it is alleged, had very little time for psychologists. In the next section I'll outline his work and seek to show its importance to the behaviourist school of psychology.

Ivan Petrovich Pavlov (1849–1936) had already earned the Nobel Prize for his work on digestion before he embarked upon the study of the physiological mechanisms of salivation. Pavlov planned to study nervous control of the digestive process, which he sought to do by measuring changes in saliva production. To do this he surgically diverted one of the ducts of the salivary gland through a special tube where it could be easily measured. It was during these experiments that some amazingly serendipitous facts emerged. To begin with, only the presence of food in the mouth would elicit marked changes in saliva production. Then it emerged that the dogs who had spent some time in the unit would salivate to previously neutral cues. Eventually the dogs would salivate to the mere sight of food, the sight of the dish in which it was placed, the sight of the person who usually brought it, and even that person's footsteps. These chance observations suggested an alternative research strategy to Pavlov and he soon switched to studying the rules of learning. Pavlov decided to see how events in the animal's life could be manipulated to change patterns of salivation. For example, Pavlov instituted a regime of buzzer sounds and food presentation such that the buzzer just preceded the presentation of food. Pavlov discovered that after having repeatedly sounded a buzzer and then presenting food for a few trials, the dogs would learn to salivate to the buzzer sound alone. Pavlov adopted the principle that the dogs were being 'conditioned' to respond to the buzzer and proposed a distinction between what he called the unconditioned and the conditioned reflex. Pavlov supposed the unconditioned reflexes to be an effectively innate reflex that would be unconditionally elicited by an appropriate stimulus irrespective of the animal's experience, such as salivating to food in the mouth. In contrast, conditioned reflexes were acquired (i.e. conditional upon the animal's experience) and therefore based upon newly formed brain connections, as was presumed to occur when the dogs were conditioned to salivate to the buzzer.

The general form of this theory, so-called 'classical conditioning' theory, and one of the basic principles of behaviourism, is that every unconditioned reflex is based upon a connection between an unconditioned stimulus (UCS) and an unconditioned response (UCR). In the above example, food-in-the-mouth is the UCS and salivation the UCR. The corresponding terms for the conditioned reflex are conditioned stimulus (CS) and conditioned response (CR). The CS is an initially neutral stimulus (here, the buzzer) that is paired with the UCS; the CR (here, again salivation) is the response elicited by the CS after some such pairings of CS and UCS. Typically, the CR is very similar to the UCR, though the two are not necessarily identical. Presenting the UCS together with, or shortly after, the CS is a critical component of classical conditioning as additional pairings further reinforce the association. Reinforcement is a further critical issue in classical conditioning and is worth exploring in a bit of detail.

Positive and negative reinforcement

A central tenet of learning theory is that behaviours can be encouraged by positive reinforcement and discouraged through the use of negative reinforcers. So what do we mean by positive and negative reinforcement? Let's stick with dog training as a medium for explaining these phenomena. Dog trainers will often reward their charges with small snacks when they have exhibited a certain type of behaviour. The notion here is that when the dog does something you like it is possible to encourage similar future behaviour by rewarding the animal with, for example, a snack, or approval. Equally, negative reinforcers such as verbal disapproval or punishment will discourage a behaviour. The challenge in using this theory is in determining what constitutes positive or negative reinforcement for the individual whose behaviour is being conditioned. A good example of this is in the management of disruptive pupils in classroom situations. Intuitively we might expect that disapproval expressed as reprimands or other forms of punishment will act as negative reinforcers. However, research has suggested that often this strategy in fact further encourages undesirable behaviour as the teacher is unwittingly providing positive reinforcement by paying the child attention! In these circumstances behaviour modification experts suggest that the teacher ignores the child, thereby failing to reward him or her for their bad behaviour.

The principles, if not the philosophy, of behaviourism, are still used in classroom behaviour modification programmes, in helping bedwetters, and in pain management clinics. This last application may come as a surprise to the reader – surely pain is the quintessential mental state? Well, not according to behaviourists, or more usually neobehaviourists. Before leaving behaviourism behind, let's consider pain from the neobehaviouristic viewpoint.

So, how do you set about explaining pain without reference to mental states? Well, actually it turns out to be very easy; one talks not of pain, but of pain behaviour. All well and good, you say, but surely this is all merely semantic sleight of hand? Not so, ripostes our behaviourism advocate who asks you to consider the following scenario.

Uncle Joe has suffered chronic intractable lower back pain since a minor accident at work. In a bid to find effective relief for this pain, Joe has been admitted to a multidisciplinary pain clinic. On admission he rates his pain at 9 out if 10, where 0 is no pain and 10 is the worst pain he can imagine. One week after admission, you turn up at the facility and ask to see Uncle Joe. The receptionist confirms that you are expected, but asks if you would first meet with the psychologist who is working with your Uncle. You are ushered into an office to meet the psychologist, who asks something very specific of you. She mentions that during previous friend and family visits she and her colleagues have observed that visitors have often carried out acts that Joe is probably quite capable of doing for himself. The psychologists suggest that, by running round after Joe, friends and family may be 'reinforcing his pain behaviour'. So here is the clue – pain is explained as pain behaviour that has been reinforced by passing Uncle Joe his stick at the first sign of a grimace from him when he reaches for the stick himself. Evidence suggests that once Joe starts doing things for himself, he will tend to rate his pain as having decreased.

There might be something missing

So, behaviourism is characterized by its reliance on observing and recording events that precipitate behaviour (the stimuli), and the elicited behaviours themselves, the responses. Conspicuously, there is no mention of, and no place for, mental life. To many psychologists forbidding explanations couched in mental terminology made psychology a very dull discipline indeed. Behaviourism denied psychologists the opportunity to talk about their favourite things, consciousness, synaesthesia, belief, etc. It took a hold simply by virtue of psychologists' desire to have their discipline accepted as a science. However, even after the acceptance of behaviourism as the dominant psychological paradigm, there was always something unsatisfying about reliance upon observable behaviour to explain why people (and other animals) do what they do. This requirement that one trusts only what one observes, rather than what one infers, leads to an odd feeling that one is perhaps missing the key element of what is interesting about psychology.

This mistrust of one's own intuition is well captured by the following joke, which for a number of years has been popular amongst psychologists.

Two behaviourist psychologists are working late one night when talk of positive reward mechanisms inflames their passions to such a degree that they rip off one another's clothes and have sex right there on the lab bench. They are both enjoying a postcoital cigarette when one turns to the other and asks, 'Well, that was good for you, but how was it for me?' A poor joke, but one that makes the point neatly.

No pain, no gain

Behaviourism fell from favour as the dominant psychological paradigm, but only after enjoying fifty years at the top. In fact, psychology has never successfully rid itself of behaviourism and even today the principles of the paradigm are used in a number of applications. Why, then, did behaviourism fall so rapidly from grace as the dominant paradigm in the late 1950s? Well, for a number of reasons, but perhaps the most damning indictment was a critique of behaviouristic explanations of language acquisition by the linguist Noam Chomsky.

BF Skinner's 'verbal behaviour'

Studying psychology soon teaches you that you cannot rely upon your intuition to inform your understanding of many psychological processes. For me the contemplation and study of language acquisition by children is a very good example of this. A folk psychological account of how children learn language would probably hold that children learn from those around them; they are, in effect, taught to speak. This appears to have been the starting point for Skinner, but he was still left with the hard part, how does this process of teaching work? Skinner supposed that children acquired language as a result of reinforcement schedules, specifically that children were more likely to repeat utterances for which they had been rewarded. Subsequent research has shown that this is unlikely for a number of reasons, but chief amongst the problems is the repeated observation that parents reward accuracy and truth over correct use of grammar. For example, a child who watches her dog leave the room and pronounces 'Elvis out goed' is more likely to be rewarded than a child who says 'Elvis has not left the building'. Skinner's theory predicts that speech would be very honest but very un-grammatical. What is remarkable is how we learn grammar; after all, most adults are insufficiently aware of the rules of grammar to teach it, and yet with sufficient exposure to language we all generally acquire the ability to speak gram-matically. Indeed, we are able to judge the grammatical correctness of a meaningless sentence. This point was made by Chomsky, who pointed out that the expression 'Colourless, green ideas sleep furiously' can be judged to be grammatically correct by individuals who have never heard the expression and who cannot provide an explanation of its meaning.

Chomsky's thorough and highly critical review of Skinner's book highlighted some of the inadequacies of the behaviourist approach, at least with respect to language acquisition. However, behaviourism was under attack from a number of sources, though ultimately the major criticism of behaviourism was that it just didn't seem likely that such a dry philosophy could be capable of capturing the full richness of human behaviour. It is not unusual to see the term behaviourism preceded by the pejorative use of 'mere'. This is unfortunate; clearly there is more in the heaven and earth of human psychology than is dreamt of in the behaviourist philosophy, but the paradigm, if not the full philosophy, is still with us.

The renaissance of cognitivism

Cognitivism appears to be back, and the rise of cognitive psychology in the1960s allowed the psychological (and neuroscientific) community to indulge once again in speculation about the nature of 'states of mind'. We have certainly enjoyed this liberty to its fullest extent, perhaps going a little too far in our contemplation of some mental states. Nevertheless, the rest of the book will be couched in terms consistent with today's dominant paradigm, cognitivism.

CHAPTER 3

Synaesthete extraordinaire?

T he cognitive revolution, or more precisely the cognitive renaissance, allowed psychologists the luxury of once again discussing what is interesting about psychology, those unseen but suspected cognitive skills. A second renaissance occurred at about the same time, the rebirth of neuropsychology, another branch of the broad church of psychology, though the cause of neuropsychology's death was very different to that of cognitive psychology. More on this later. The science of synaesthesia discussed in this chapter shares much in common with the methodology of neuropsychology, a similarity described in the next section.

The power of one

You might recall that in the last chapter it was suggested that the synaesthesia literature of the late nineteenth and early twentieth centuries was necessarily composed of case study reports, primarily because inferential statistics had not yet been developed? This is the main reason, but perhaps a greater barrier to reporting on groups of synaesthetes was the paucity of data. After all, synaesthetes appear to be fairly few and far between; according to our research, the figure is as few as 0.0005% of the population. This was also a restriction on the activities of neuropsychologists who investigated the cognitive abilities of individuals who had suffered brain injury. This sounds an odd occupation; why would looking at brain-injured individuals tell us about normal cognitive processes? Well, its not as silly as it sounds, and, because we will need to draw on the methodology used by neuropsychologists later in the chapter, the next few sections will briefly describe the history and methodology of neuropsychology.

Getting one's bumps felt

Early in the nineteenth century a famous debate was played out by two key figures in European science, each of whom propounded a very different view of brain function. The first of these protagonists was the French physiologist Pierre Flourens (1794–1867). Flourens believed that the various components of the cortex were equipotential in that they could, in principle, all carry out any cognitive function. In the red corner stood the figure of Franz Josef Gall (1758–1828) who took a very different view. Gall, an anatomist by trade, believed that cognitive faculties could be localized to discrete cortical areas. Physiological evidence collected during the early part of the nineteenth century suggested that Flourens was correct. Nevertheless, Gall retained a large element of support, which he exploited and popularized through his 'science of phrenology'. As we shall see later in this chapter, evidence acquired in the second half of the nineteenth century tended to support Gall's localizationist view.

Gall and other phrenologists made a living by literally feeling the skulls of their clients to determine their cognitive profile. Gall became fêted at the courts of Europe for his claimed ability to determine the extent to which individual

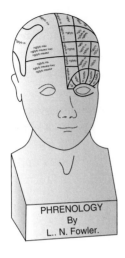

Figure 6 Phrenological head by LN Fowler. This is Lorenzo Niles Fowler's (1811–1896) guide to the bumps. It seems that phrenology retained some respectability, so much so that Fowler was invited to assess 'Ginqua', the leader of the Amistad rebels. Fowler reported his findings in the *American Phreno-logical Journal* and *Miscellany* (1840 Volume 2, 136–38), in which he describes 'Ginqua' in the following terms: 'Mr. Editor – Inasmuch as the Africans, recently cast upon our shore, have created considerable excitement in various parts of the country, I have thought it might be interesting to present the public, through your Journal, with a brief sketch of the phrenological developments and character of their leader, viz. Joseph Cinquez or Ginqua. On the 5th of September, I visited New Haven, where the Africans were then confined, and made a critical examination of Cinquez's head. I also took in plaster of Paris an exact likeness of his head, which is now deposited in my cabinet, and may be examined by any person who will call at No. 135 Nassau Street, New York. The following cut, taken from this cast, will perhaps convey to your readers a correct view of the outlines of Cinquez's head. His head is peculiar in shape, being long and high, but narrow. The base of his brain is inferior in size; consequently the lower animal propensities do not constitute the leading elements of his character. His temperament is very favourable to mental and physical exercise, being nervous bilious, with a fair portion of the sanguine. He is rather tall and spare, but well-formed, and adapted for great physical and mental exertions. His appearance indicates a strong constitution, and great powers of endurance. He has very fine pliable hair, thin and soft skin, with strongly-marked nervous and locomotive powers. His head measures most in the region of those faculties giving a love of liberty, independence, determination, ambition, regard for his country, and for what he thinks is sacred and right; also, good practical talents and powers of observation, shrewdness, tact, and management, joined with an uncommon degree of moral courage and pride of character'.

clients possessed various mental skills. The assumption made by Gall was that distinct brain areas housed different abilities (Figure 6) and so a large bump above an area indicated high ability whereas a smaller bump suggested less skill.

We now know that the function to structure claims made by phrenologists have very dubious legitimacy. However, the notion that various brain areas subserve different cognitive skills was given some legitimacy by scientists working several years after Gall began feeling aristocratic convolutions.

The birth of neuropsychology

By the middle of the nineteenth century it had been known for some time by clinicians and scientists alike that apparently specific impairments could be seen in patients who had suffered brain injury. However, what remained obscure was the relationship between the location of the injury and the observed deficit. Towards the end of the nineteenth century some headway was made with this issue, and many commentators have suggested that a seminal moment in this was the work published in 1861 by the French clinician Paul Broca (1824–1880).

Broca knew that post-mortem examinations of individuals who in life had lost their capacity to speak tended to reveal that damage to the left side of the brain had occurred. However, it was only when Broca met a patient whose only verbal ability was to say 'tan' that he was able to locate speech production to a specific brain area.

Broca's patient had suffered a brain lesion that had left him mute, except for the ability to say a single word, a disability that led to him being named 'Tan'. Unfortunately for

Tan, after meeting Broca he died and came to Broca's post-mortem slab as an individual whose cognitive abilities appeared to be intact, save his capacity to produce speech. Broca wasted no time in displaying Tan's remains – his brain was on show at a meeting the day after he died! Broca's post-mortem examination revealed a very specific finding. The only damaged region of Tan's brain was the third frontal convolution of the left hemisphere, an area subsequently known as 'Broca's area'. Broca continued collecting cases of aphasia and observed that damage always seemed to occur in much the same brain region. It is, as Broca said at the time, that 'nous parlons avec l'hemisphere gauche'. This is the principle by which a number of neuro-psychologists work, i.e. look for evidence of cognitive disability and brain injury. In this way a connection between cognition (function) and anatomy (structure) can be established.

Modularity and dissociation

From the example of Broca's work it is perhaps obvious that the opportunity for neuropsychologists working with brain-damaged patients is to show that one area of cognition can be compromised in the absence of deficits in other cognitive domains. In the case of Broca's patient, the ability to speak is selectively damaged and, in neuro-psychological parlance, is therefore described as being 'dissociable'. From a neuropsychological point of view the cognitive ability of producing speech might be described as modular in that it is a 'stand alone' component of a normal individual's cognition.

So are other cognitive skills dissociable? Is it possible, for example, to find brain-injured patients who have other

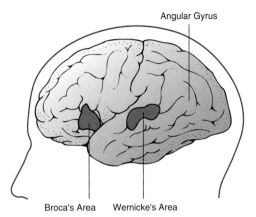

Figure 7 Positions of Broca's area, Wernicke's area, and the angular gyrus.

circumscribed deficits? The work of scientists seeking to link function to structure suggests it is. In fact, only 13 years after Broca localized speech production a German scientist, Carl Wernicke (1848–1905), reported that, according to his observations, an area of the temporal lobes appeared to be crucial to the comprehension of speech. These observations provided evidence that speech production and comprehension were both dissociable and modular, and that damage to Broca's area would cause the former, whereas the latter was caused by damage to Wernicke's area. The fact that speech production and comprehension deficits can be found in isolation in different individuals provides neuropsychologists with a 'double dissociation', the strongest evidence for localization of these two cognitive functions.

'Head' and 'brain'

The implication of Broca and Wernicke's work is that damage to their eponymous brain areas will lead to either sensory aphasia (absence of speech comprehension) or production aphasia (absence of speech production). This is neat science, highly predictive and easily testable – which is why it was easy to test and, unfortunately, equally easy to refute.

A curiosity of neurology in the early part of the twentieth century is the frequency with which eminent figures in the field possessed names entirely applicable to their professions. Many of us will have met Dr Pains in our time, but few will have met neurologists named Head or Brain. Henry Head was a very forthright man who was struck by the mounting contrary evidence to the neat function–structure relationships posited by Broca, Wernicke, and their followers. Some of this contrary evidence had extended to a reanalysis of the cases upon which Broca had localized the brain region responsible for speech production. This work, reported by Marie in 1906, suggested that the lesions extended considerably beyond the area delineated by Broca. Head also pointed out that it was possible to have aphasia in the absence of damage to either Broca's or Wernicke's areas. Yet others had shown that damage to these areas did not necessarily lead to either production or sensory aphasia. In a fatal blow to the diagrams of aphasia structure–function created by the first wave of neuropsychologists, Head announced in 1926 that 'The time was ripe for a ruthless destruction of false gods'. Head's dolorous blow proved fatal and localizationist neuropsychology fell from favour and prominence. However, lest we throw the baby out with the bathwater, it is indeed often the case that damage to Broca's area leads to production aphasia. Like so many laws of behavioural neuroscience, it is probably more true than it is not. The same would hold for the relationship between sensory aphasia and damage to Wernicke's area, i.e. it is not an invariant relationship, but it is often found to be the case.

Functional? Or is it just in the plumbing?

The notion that neurological function and neural structure neatly compartmentalize into convenient modules may also be more true than not. It is sometimes possible to show that cognitive and neural modules map in a relatively neat one-to-one relationship. However, assuming too much modularity might dangerously mislead us. The dangers of this approach are discussed in more detail in Chapter 6. However, in advance of this it is convenient to illustrate briefly the dangers of too rigid a belief in neat modular mapping here, an issue addressed with a discussion of the collection of signs and symptoms collectively known as Gerstmann's syndrome.

This syndrome, named after the neurologist who first posited the existence of the syndrome, refers to a combination of four neurological signs held to co-occur as the consequence of lesions to the angular gyrus of the left hemisphere (Figure 7):

- *Finger agnosia* – an impairment of identifying different fingers of the same hand.
- *Agraphia* – the loss of the ability to write.
- *Acalculia* – loss of the ability to carry out arithmetic.
- *Left/right confusion.*

Gerstmann proposed that all four signs were due to a single lesion and, further, that all four signs were caused by damage to a single cognitive module, or 'Grundstorung'. The debate as to how likely that either of these two theses is correct has run ever since they were first published in 1924. Counter evidence includes the observation that it is possible to suffer damage to the left angular gyrus without suffering so much as one of these deficits. Equally, damage in brain areas other than the angular gyrus can cause these four difficulties. However, the critical issues for us in the consideration of Gerstmann's syndrome is whether there is a direct mapping between damage to a specific structural module and a single functional module. A number of scientists have pointed out that it is not at all obvious what single cognitive skill could be compromised and then lead to four such different cognitive deficits. Other commentators have pointed out that angular gyrus damage can lead to just one, two, or three of the signs reported to make up the syndrome.

An alternative explanation is that damage to the left angular gyrus can disrupt the operation of several cognitive functions, some of which subserve writing skills, others arithmetic, and yet others the ability to tell left from right. That these signs often co-occur is due to the proximity of their neural substrates within the territory of the angular gyrus. Until recently the weight of opinion was against the notion that Gerstmann's syndrome was because of deficits in a single Grundstorung. However, a recent publication has suggested that the single cognitive deficit might be impairment in the mental manipulation of images.

Mapping function to structure is thus not without its hazards, a theme we will revisit later in this chapter. There are other hazards in linking function to structure which are also worthy of some brief consideration.

How reliable is localization of function? Further difficulties

Probably the most challenging aspect of working as a jobbing neuropsychologist is the scarcity of study material.

Unfortunately brain injury is usually a very messy affair. Injury caused by infection is often widely distributed across a number of brain areas. Open head injury, such as might be caused by a blow to the head, often causes injury local to the point of the skull where the impact occurred. However, blows to the head can also cause the brain to jerk violently in the cerebrospinal fluid (CSF) in which it floats. These violent shifts can cause nerves to suffer shearing injury at sites throughout the brain. Blows to the head can also cause the brain to collide with the skull because of the physical force of the blow. The collision of the brain with the skull can cause so-called contre-coup injuries at locations on the other side of the brain from the location of the blow.

So-called closed head injuries caused by stroke are also usually quite messy affairs, typically leading to fairly widespread damage and consequent loss of function. Strokes cause brain damage either by obstructing bloodflow, leading to oxygen deprivation 'downstream' (ischaemic stroke), or by the leakage of blood into surrounding territory (haemorrhagic stroke). Sometimes the ischaemic or haemorrhagic damage is relatively limited so that only a small amount of brain damage occurs. This can also occur in instances of open head injury as suffered by the only case known to us of a synaesthete who lost his synaesthesia as the result of brain injury.

A (the) neuropsychology of synaesthesia?

The visual system has received a great deal of attention from all branches of neuroscience. As with most areas of neuroscience, controversy still exists with regard to most interpretations of the available data. However, what has been proven to the satisfaction of most observers is that it is possible to lose certain aspects of vision while retaining others, i.e. the components of vision are 'dissociable'. For example, within the neuropsychological literature there are documented cases of the following:

- Patients who cannot determine what an object is (agnosia), but who can still see colour and motion.
- Individuals who retain their ability to see colour and form, but who have lost their ability to see movement (akinetopsia).

Other reported cases contain accounts of individuals who have lost their ability to see colour (achromatopsia), but retain their ability to see form and movement. Just such a case was reported by the well known neurologist Oliver Sacks and his coworkers. Their patient, known as convention demands by his initials (JI), was involved in a car accident that caused what at the time appeared to be relatively minor injuries. However, as a result of this accident JI reported that he had lost his ability to see colour. As a painter this constituted a devastating loss, but what is of major interest to us is that until his accident JI enjoyed sound colour synaesthesia. Also of significance for us is that JI also found that he now no longer experienced dreams in colour. The significance of this finding will be revisited in the next chapter. Unfortunately, no reliable anatomical information is available about this patient, who died 3 years after the accident (S Zeki, personal communication). However, on the basis of our knowledge of other cases of achromatopsia it is most likely that JI suffered damage to the lingual and fusiform gyri of the brain (Figure 8).

JI suffered brain damage as the result of a car accident and as a consequence became cortically colour blind ('achromatopsic'). However, when JI lost his ability to see

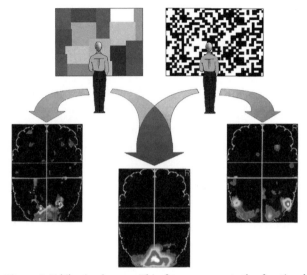

Figure 8 Zeki's visual areas. This figure represents the functional specialization known to occur in human visual processing areas. Colour processing occurs in the human V4 area and the processing of motion occurs in human V5. All retinally derived visual stimuli are processed by primary visual areas V1 and V2. See also Plate 1. Reproduced with permission of La Recherche.

colour, he also lost his colour hearing synaesthesia as well as his ability to dream in colour. Such a pattern of dysfunction opens up the possibility that these capacities may share a common neural substrate.

The power of one – part two – 'synaesthete extraordinaire'

The single cases we have considered so far have been cases where function has been lost as the consequence of brain injury. JI is slightly unusual in that one of the abilities he lost as a result of his accident was supranormal, namely his synaesthesia. In this last section I shall describe the single participant who began Baron-Cohen's investigations into synaesthesia, then a 76-year-old professional painter who trained at the Chelsea School of Art in the 1930s named Elizabeth Stewart-Jones.

Elizabeth came to Baron-Cohen's attention as a result of placing an advertisement in the journal of the British Psychological Society in which she described herself as:

> An artist who has experienced the life-long condition of hearing words and sounds in colour.

This description piqued Baron-Cohen's curiosity, so much so that he invited Elizabeth to visit him at his offices at the Institute of Psychiatry in London.

Baron-Cohen was fascinated but concerned as to how he might satisfy himself and then others that there was anything of interest in Elizabeth's description. As a fully trained clinical psychologist he knew there were several steps he could sensibly take to be more certain that Elizabeth genuinely saw words in colour. Let me stress again here that it is not that psychologists necessarily distrust what study participants tell them, simply that the 'burden of proof' requires that data is collected that will persuade others. These steps were:

- Check for current or past psychiatric or neurological disorder.
- Check for previous drug use.
- Conduct a brief neuropsychological test assessment.

No evidence was found of any disorder and Elizabeth reported no history of drug abuse. These issues are both very important because there are accounts of LSD users seeing music. Equally, there is published anecdotal evidence of individuals with schizophrenia describing synaesthesic perceptions. These issues are both discussed in some detail later in the book.

The neuropsychological assessment was a critical component of the assessment as it was important for the purposes of the study to determine whether Elizabeth's other cognitive skills were good, bad, or indifferent. For this reason Elizabeth was assessed with the following psychological tests:

1. The Wechsler adult intelligence scale – revised (WAIS-R) is an extensively used test of intelligence. The scale is composed of 11 subtests so that different intelligence skills (e.g. 'arithmetic', 'verbal', 'performance') can be independently measured. Good estimates of IQ can be obtained by administering just a few of these subtests. Elizabeth was examined on four subtests:

- Vocabulary – participants are asked to provide word definitions, starting with items such as 'breakfast' and working up to harder words such as 'tirade'.

- Similarities – in this subtest the participant is asked to explain in what sense two objects are similar. For example, the subject is asked 'In what way are a boat and a car alike?'

- Picture completion – this test requires the participant to examine an incomplete picture and report what is missing. In one picture, for example, a pair of glasses has been drawn without the nosepiece.

- Block design – in this test participants are given small blocks with faces that are either completely red, completely white, or split between the two. They are then shown progressively more complex designs that they are asked to reproduce by assembling the small blocks.

2. The Wechsler memory scale – revised (WMS-R) is from the same stable as the WAIS-R and, as the name implies, is designed to test different aspects of memory. Two of the WMS-R subtests were selected to administer to Elizabeth:

- Design recall – this assesses the participant's ability to recall a series of abstract designs from memory.
- Logical memory – this is a test of the participant's ability to remember verbal material; in the case of this test, two short stories.

3. The Farnsworth-Munsell 100 hue test is designed to assess how accurately the participant can discriminate coloured blocks that are progressively, but only slightly, different hues from one another.

Baron-Cohen also included a bespoke test of **object recognition memory**, in which the participant is shown 12 photographs of an object and asked to study them. Later, the same photographs are represented but are this time accompanied by a second and slightly different view of the same objects. The participant is asked to pick which of the two views they originally studied. Whereas the WMS-R tasks were tests of recall, this test, because the original 'to-be-remembered-item' is present at the testing phase, is known as a recognition memory test.

A key issue in the use of tests with individual participants is how one determines their level of performance. This question raises issues that have implications for the analysis of experimental data described later in the book. For this reason the next section describes how psychologists decide how good, or bad, a score is.

How to decide if a test score is unusually good or bad

Testing a participant to obtain a measure of their ability is all very well, but it is only meaningful in the context of how good or bad their performance is by comparison with what one might normally expect. Psychologists have adopted statistical methods of deciding whether a score is unusually good or unusually bad and in this section I shall describe the method most often used.

The normal distribution

Statisticians are generally concerned with the collection of measurement data and finding useful ways of describing results. Data are literally a group of individual observations. An interesting and useful characteristic of many kinds of data is that, when data points are ordered by frequency, they tend to exhibit a reliable pattern of distribution. A tried and trusted example is the distribution of the height of males in the UK, in which the average height turns out to be about 5'7". To obtain this average, or, in statistical parlance, 'mean' height, it is necessary to measure a group of UK males, add all their heights together and then divide by the number of men in your group. To be absolutely sure that your calculated mean height is accurate you would need to measure the height of every man in the UK, which is clearly more bother than it is worth. To avoid having to do this we take what we hope is a representative sample from the population, obtain the mean height of this group, and use this as an estimate of the mean height of the population.

As well as calculating the mean it is also helpful to know how much the population varies from the mean. The statistic usually calculated in science to describe variance is the standard deviation, or SD for short. A description of how the SD is calculated is more than a little dry and beyond the remit of this book. All we need to know is that calculating the SD gives us a measure of how much the population varies around the mean, and that the SD can be used by

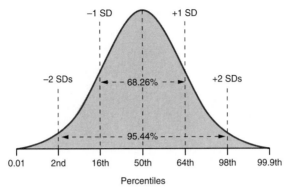

Figure 9 The normal or 'Gaussian' distribution with standard deviation/percentile equivalent scores.

psychologists to make judgements about whether performance is relatively good or bad.

Figure 9 is a histogram which has frequency plotted on the vertical axis (*y* axis or ordinate*). The horizontal (*x* axis or abscissa†) axis is unlabelled but could in fact be any dataset, the height of the UK male population included.

This bell-shaped distribution often occurs when datasets are plotted by frequency, so much so that this pattern is referred to as the 'normal' distribution. It is also sometimes described as the Gaussian distribution after its discoverer, the German mathematician Carl Gauss (1777–1855). A remarkable and extremely useful property of this distribution is that for any normally distributed dataset, approximately 66% of all data will fall between one standard deviation above or below the mean. Also, approximately 96% of all the data will fall between the minus two SD point and

---

*From the Latin *Linea ordinate* (a line applied in an orderly manner).
†From the Latin *Linea Abscissa* ('a cut-off of a line').

the plus two SD point. This leaves 2% of the data at the top end of the distribution and 2% at the bottom end.

Two standard deviations below the mean is the point at which psychologists would define a score as being abnormal. However, this is not a pejorative use of the term abnormal; it is merely meant to show that such a score would not fall in the 'normal range', defined as 2 SDs above or below the mean. Thus an individual scoring in the top 2% would also be described as abnormal, as their score would also fall outside of the normal range. This methodology is best illustrated with the use of a real example, so let's use it to determine how well Elizabeth performed on the four WAIS-R tests.

Test\Percentile	2nd	5th	16th	37th	50th	63rd	84th	95th	98th
Vocabulary									X
Similarities								X	
Picture completion							X		
Block design									X

The table shown above lists the adopted Wechsler tests in the first column. In successive columns are percentile score possibilities and the column appropriate to Elizabeth's performance is marked with an X. As you can see, her performance is considerably better than average (50th percentile), in two cases qualifying as extremely good.

It is a matter of chance

So what does it mean to say that two SDs below the mean is the threshold for abnormally poor performance? Another way to express it is to say that the probability of any individual scoring at or below this level is about 1 in 20. Thus the assumption being made is that there is a reason why an individual would score at this level. In the case of a patient with brain injury, test performance at the -2 SD level would be assumed to be because of their injury. It is worth pointing out that many psychologists argue that when dealing with brain-injured individuals, they have no expectation of showing test improvement. Consequently the abnormally good group of approximately 2% at the top end of the distribution is redundant as they have no expectation of such high levels of performance. To accommodate this psychologists shift the abnormality range to the right of the distribution and declare individual test performance to be abnormal if the score falls in the bottom 5%. This figure also has significance in the comparison of group performance that will be discussed in the next chapter. Let us now return to the other assessments that were carried out on Elizabeth during her visit to the Institute of Psychiatry.

Check the waves

Baron-Cohen also checked for any suggestion of unusual brain activity and asked a colleague, Dr Colin Binnie, to carry out an electroencephalogram (EEG) assessment (see Chapter 1). These test procedures were all relatively easy to carry out. What was much less easy to determine was how to obtain evidence that Elizabeth really did experience coloured hearing synaesthesia, a need that required, and obtained, an elegant solution.

The rise of cognitivism has for the most part been an emancipating experience for psychologists. However, it has also been an excellent reminder of the challenges that drove psychologists into the arms of behaviourism. One of the most challenging issues for cognitive psychologists and neuroscientists has been to find methods of providing objective evidence for the existence of subjectively experienced 'mental' states. Put more simply, whilst individuals may tell us that they perceive colour on hearing sound, in order to evaluate the scientific merit of the condition scientists require hard objective evidence. This same challenge faces scientists seeking to understand phenomena such as hallucinations and consciousness, mental states for which objective confirmation is hard to come by. This issue is revisited again in later chapters and especially in the chapter dealing with brain imaging (Chapter 6).

The solution arrived at by Baron-Cohen and his colleagues has been repeatedly applied in our research and has been a key method of confirming as genuine the cases that have been investigated. The test has evolved in the course of the last few years, but has remained essentially the same. It will be described in some detail later in this chapter, but before doing so we will consider some important issues relevant to the design of good psychological tests.

Reliability and 'rubber rulers'

A key issue in the construction of psychological tests is the issue of reliability. Test reliability has a number of different facets. For example, one might wonder whether the same individual tested by two different examiners would yield the same outcome. This form of reliability is described as 'inter-rater' reliability. A related issue is whether the same examiner testing the same participant would necessarily obtain the same score, so-called 'intra-rater' reliability. However, a key issue regarding the reliability of a psychological test is what is described as 'test–retest' reliability.

Your own experience of trying to learn a new skill is probably that 'practice makes perfect'. Tasks vary in their degree of difficulty; some are so easy to learn that just one exposure

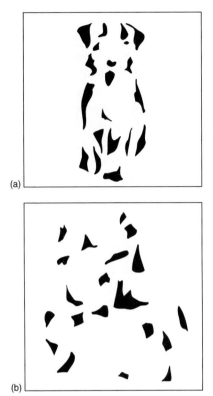

(a)

(b)

Figure 10 Ambiguous figure. What do these degraded images suggest to you? Most people fairly readily recognize the uppermost figure as a dog, but the lower figure usually takes a little longer. However, once the horse and rider have been seen, it is almost impossible not to see them immediately when shown the figure again.

will mean that the task will be trivially easy the second time. Take, for example, the pictures shown in Figure 10. Take a look at the pictures before you read on.

You probably quite readily identified the dog. It may have taken you some time to see it, or, if you have seen it before, you probably picked it out immediately. However, the mounted horse may have taken you a little longer, or perhaps eluded you entirely? Look back at the figure; if your experience is like mine it is now impossible *not* to see the dog and the horse and rider. Thus if this picture were to be used as a test of visual perception your performance second time around (retest) would have been heavily influenced by your first exposure (test). This difficulty is a major issue in psychological test construction – how to measure cognition reliably without allowing the results to be influenced by previous experience. Contrast this type of measurement with our previous example of measuring the height of adult males. If you measure the same male on two consecutive days at about the same time of day, barring major physical trauma you would expect to obtain much the same measurement on both occasions, thus your testing method for obtaining height is, if you will forgive the poor pun, highly reliable. It is hard to imagine that any psychological test can be perfectly reliable; the issue is one of degree – tests are either more or less reliable than one another. The metaphor for psychometric tests is that they are 'rubber rulers' in that their ability to measure accurately is imperfect. A contrast is often drawn between 'psychometric' and 'biometric' measurement (an example of the latter would be the measurement of height). However, it is worth pointing out that a number of biometric tests enjoy less than perfect test–retest reliability, blood pressure measurement being a good example. Good psychological tests need to be reliable, both from an administration standpoint (intra- and inter-rater reliability) and in terms of their ability to measure reliably from occasion to occasion. Let us consider this issue in the context of the solution arrived at by Baron-Cohen and his colleagues in testing Elizabeth Stewart-Jones' synaesthesia.

The 'test of genuineness'

Test–retest or 'temporal' reliability is usually determined by assessing a number of individuals on two separate occasions and then looking to see how related each participant's performance was at timepoint 1 (test) and timepoint 2 (retest). In fact, we are looking to see how co-related the two sets of scores are, or, in statistical parlance, how correlated they are. Let us say, for example, that we asked a group of synaesthetes to tell us what colours they saw when we read them a list of different words. As we saw in Chapter 2, while synaesthetes seldom agree with one another about a word's colour, the word–colour correspondence for any individual synaesthete is unchanging. Consequently we would expect them to be extremely accurate in their description at both test and retest. But what about the performance of control (i.e. non-synaesthetic) individuals who have been asked to link a colour with a word? There is no reason why they should be particularly consistent, unless, of course, they possess extremely good memories. It could be that words in the list suggest a colour association. For example, the word 'snow' may well conjure an automatic association with white, 'blood' with red, 'coal' with black, etc. So, while we might expect the performance of control participants and synaesthetes to be very different, they might also be expected to score consistently from test to retest.

This is precisely the logic adopted by Baron-Cohen and his colleagues – the 'test of genuineness' is in fact no more than a list of more than 100 words and letters given to participants on two occasions. On the first occasion ('baseline') the colour correspondences/associations are noted down and then compared for similarity with the descriptions given at retest. The version of the test of genuineness given to Elizabeth was composed of words from the following categories of words:

Animals (10)

Place names (10)

Objects (10)

Occupations (10)

Abstract terms (10)

Days of the week (7)

Christian names (20)

The letters of the alphabet (26).

Elizabeth was also asked to describe colours for nonsense 'pseudowords' selected to have a 60% similarity to real words (e.g. 'HUK', 'SAH', etc.).

Baron-Cohen and his colleagues reasoned that if the colour–word correspondences were reliably consistent then Elizabeth should, when retested, effortlessly be able to reproduce the same descriptions that she had previously provided. However, they were also keen to establish how well a non-synaesthete would perform when asked to provide colour descriptions at the test and phase and then recall these descriptions at retest. Consequently, a 27-year-old woman of superior intelligence and an excellent memory was recruited and tested using a similar protocol to that used with Elizabeth. The only protocol differences were that the control participant was encouraged to use memory strategies for associating words with colours, and she was retested only 2 weeks after the first test.

The design of the experiment required that colour descriptions of each of the words in the test of genuineness were collected for both participants as a baseline for future comparisons. Then both participants were tested 3 hours later on 10 of the test items, randomly selected from the original word list. Elizabeth and the control participant were then tested for a second time 10 weeks after the baseline data had been collected. The team could now compare both participants' original descriptions with those made 3 hours and 10 or 2 weeks later to see how similar they were. This methodology allowed for a quantitative assessment to be made; however, just as interesting were the qualitative aspects of the data, especially regarding the detail of the colour descriptions.

There were marked obvious differences in the degree of detail provided by Elizabeth and by the control participant. The control participant tended to give fairly simple, single primary colour associations for the words in the test of genuineness, whereas Elizabeth's descriptions were highly detailed. The following three examples neatly illustrate the relative complexity of Elizabeth's colour–word correspondences:

- Moscow – darkish grey, with spinach-green and pale blue in places.
- Fear – mottled light grey, with a touch of soft green and purple.
- Daniel – is deep purple, blue, and red, and is shiny.

Clearly, these are quite complex descriptions and therefore presumably not particularly easy to remember and recall. Evidence in support of this assertion can be mustered from the performance of the control participant who, in spite of providing comparatively simpler descriptions, could only accurately recall 17% at 2 week retest. Elizabeth's performance was quite extraordinarily good; she was able to reproduce the colour descriptions with precise and absolute accuracy, in spite of not having been pre-warned that she would be retested.

Baron-Cohen also sought to investigate the consequences of presenting Elizabeth with an unfamiliar word. What, for example, did Elizabeth describe for a pseudoword such as HUK? The answer turned out to be quite simple. As well as each word having a consistent specific set of colour correspondences, so too did each letter of her alphabet. Consequently, HUK was described as being composed of:

H – dark red

U – yellow

K – purple.

Two plus two equals seven

Elizabeth's letter-by-letter description of the pseudoword HUK might be expected to provide a key to the colour correspondences for other words containing these letters. After all, if colour–word correspondences were based on an association of a colour with each letter in the alphabet this would be a very simple way to reproduce descriptions made at baseline testing. However, what is extraordinary about Elizabeth, and what marks her apart from any other synaesthete we have ever tested, is that it appears to be impossible to predict the colour correspondence of a word based on her colour–letter associations. In the original paper Baron-Cohen and his colleagues point out that the words man, moon, moan, mean all have very different colour correspondences.

Couldn't it just be that synaesthetes are possessed of extremely able memories?

An oft-heard question, and in fairness this could be the case. There are some facts that argue against such an explanation, but this would easily qualify as the most parsimonious explanation. This, of course, does not fit with Elizabeth's conscious experience of her synaesthesia, but the issue in science is to satisfy the most sceptically minded individuals. Note that the perspective being offered here is not that synaesthetes are deliberately seeking to mislead us, simply that they may be recalling colour associations that they are not aware of having previously learnt. With regard to this issue it is worth remembering that when Elizabeth's memory skills were formally tested her performance was competent, but otherwise unremarkable. Nevertheless, it could be argued that her memory for colour–word correspondences has been more highly developed. We should be willing to accept that Elizabeth's prodigious capacity to recall detailed descriptions perfectly for 103 words may be due to an extraordinarily good memory. It is of course worth remembering that Elizabeth was not warned that she would be retested, but even in spite of this an amazing memory might be the obvious explanation, even though she herself denies this.

In an interesting reversal of this argument a figure often described as a synaesthete was the Russian mnemonist Solomon Veniaminóvitch Shereshevski, the subject of a recent Peter Brook play entitled *Je suis un phénomène*. In the next section of this chapter this case is described as the last example of a behavioural study of a single case, though we shall return to single case studies in a later chapter on brain imaging (Chapter 6).

The mind of a mnemonist

You might remember that during our consideration of the normal distribution it was pointed out that beyond the normal range lie the abnormally 'poor' and, at the other end, the abnormally good? Most neuropsychologists concern themselves exclusively with the study of individuals who are found in the bottom 2%. However, a famous Russian neuropsychologist, Alexandr Romanóvitch Luria, made it his habit to study both ends of the distribution. Luria contributed hugely to our understanding of the effects of brain injury upon cognition. However, he probably remains best known for the account of his friend, the subject of Luria's book *The Mind of a Mnemonist*, a 30-year study of a man with the most extraordinary memory.

Total recall

Solomon Veniaminóvitch Shereshevski appears to have forgotten nothing. According to Luria's account, Shereshevski, or S, could effortlessly recall information. In Luria's words he had a memory 'Which for all practical purposes was inexhaustible'. Luria conducted a long series of experiments with S and reported that a table of 50 unrelated digits could be encoded in no more than 3 minutes and then perfectly reproduced in just 40 seconds.

As well as these phenomenal feats of memory, Luria also reports details of S's synaesthesia. A series of carefully controlled experiments were conducted at the Russian Academy of Medical Sciences. These tests were designed to show how changes in pitch and amplitude influenced the synaesthesic percepts experienced by S. Examples from this experiment are shown in the following table.

Luria records that these same stimuli were delivered on a variety of other occasions and always elicited the same descriptions from S. Voices, too, seemed to have distinctive synaesthesic characteristics for S. On one occasion, S comments to Vygotsky, a famous Russian psychologist, 'What a crumbly, yellow voice you have'. S also met the Russian film

Pitch (Hz)	Amplitude (db)	Percept
30	100	A strip of 12–15 cm in width the colour of old tarnished silver
50	100	A brown strip on a dark background with red tongue-like edges
100	86	A wide-strip, reddish-orange in the centre and gradually fading to pink at the edges
250	64	A velvet cord of a pleasant pink–orange hue
500	74	A dense, orange colour
500	100	A streak of lightning splitting the heavens in two
2000	113	Fireworks tinged with a pink–red hue
3000	128	A fiery colour

director Sergei Eisenstein, whose voice he describes as being 'as though a flame with fibres protruding from it was advancing right towards me'. Eisenstein is also sometimes described as being a synaesthete, and so it is of interest that S met him. The supposed synaesthesia of famous figures is discussed again in Chapter 5.

There are clearly some mismatches between Baron-Cohen's account of Elizabeth's cognitions and those of S. You might recall that Elizabeth's verbal memory was entirely normal, but otherwise unremarkable. From Luria's account of S it is hard to imagine that he would have failed to recall any part of the Wechsler logical memory tests. It seems likely that S would pass any test of genuineness, perhaps because of his astonishing memory. The question in S's case is 'was his memory good because he was a synaesthete?', or, 'was his capacity to use imagery to recall so rich that it sounded like he was a synaesthete?' S is sadly no longer with us and provides us with a slightly melancholy close to this chapter, for it seems that his inability to forget proved too much for him, so much so that he took his own life.

Let us now move on to the study of groups of synaesthetes and leave the study of single cases behind for a few chapters.

CHAPTER 4

The closet door opens

As an undergraduate I had the good fortune to be placed at the Institute of Psychiatry in London's Denmark Hill, located close to the Maudsley Hospital, a centre known and respected throughout the world. I also had the excellent good fortune to be supervised by Dr Laura Goldstein, a clinical psychologist whose guidance and supervision during that summer proved invaluable. My lowly student status meant that I could not, for insurance reasons, test patients. I would therefore not get the chance to gain first hand experience of psychological testing. However, Laura found a means by which I could gain experience of testing, chiefly as a result of some research conducted by her office mate, Dr Simon Baron-Cohen.

Dr Goldstein had arranged a fascinating programme of work for me. I had the chance to watch her conduct psychological assessments of patients with damage to their central nervous systems. I was also allowed to attend case conferences of patients who appeared to have pseudoepileptic seizures and those with the fascinating, though often debilitating, neuropsychological syndromes I had thus far only read about. This was all amazing enough, but more extraordinary experiences were in store for me. One of the two most amazing experiences I had was to watch a 'Wada' procedure. The candidate for this procedure had been admitted to the neurosurgery unit to have a slow growing tumour removed from the temporal lobe on the left side of his brain. The location of this tumour was such that surgery might well have deprived him of crucial memory and language abilities. However, the team dealing with this patient knew that it was often the case that the right hemisphere also housed these skills and so it was extremely useful to determine how cognitively competent the right side of a patient's brain could be. One way to establish this is to anaesthetize the left half of the brain and then test the cognitive skills of the still awake right hemisphere. This procedure, first conducted by Dr Wada, required that a line be fed into the femoral artery and then up the carotid artery that provides the left half of the brain with oxygenated blood. Once this line has been successfully inserted, sodium pentathol or sodium amytal is fed through the line to anaesthetize just that half of the brain. While 'half asleep' the still conscious right hemisphere of the brain can be tested to determine the extent of its cognitive competence. The image of the patient's right arm 'falling asleep' once the anaesthesia took, while the left arm remained functional, will live with me forever! However, I digress. Let me now turn to the second fascinating opportunity I was given, testing people with synaesthesia.

Science on 4

A major issue in conducting experimentation is the recruitment of study participants. It is hard enough to obtain normal control participants – recruiting individuals with a condition as rare as we believed synaesthesia to be would ordinarily be extremely challenging. Fortunately, Baron-Cohen had recently received correspondence from a number of individuals who all claimed to have the condition, many of whom were willing to be tested.

There has been a great deal of media coverage of our work in the last decade and each time something has been published we have heard from new synaesthetes. However, we have never enjoyed as dramatic a response as that received by Simon Baron-Cohen as a consequence of the *Science on 4* programme. The study of Elizabeth Stewart-Jones had been picked up by the people at *Science on 4*, a still popular radio programme in which interesting pieces of contemporary science are reported. *Science on 4* had invited Simon and Elizabeth to talk about synaesthesia and, at the end of the programme, listeners were invited to write in if they believed themselves to be synaesthetes. A whopping 212 letters were received, to which replies were sent, along with a questionnaire to complete. Levels of motivation in these individuals were staggeringly high and there was considerable interest in volunteering for further experiments. To my huge good fortune, a sample of individuals with coloured hearing for all sounds was willing to volunteer their time and agreed to visit me at the Institute for testing. I am eternally grateful to them for their cooperation.

Experimental design

This second study utilized much of the design used in Simon's study of Elizabeth described in Chapter 3, but this time we had the advantage of being able to analyse our results with inferential group statistics. We also had the opportunity to make our experimental design a little more robust by including new provisions to make detecting an effect as stringent as possible. The key outcome measure was still to be the Test of Genuineness, but this time we added a few more items to make the test 130 items long. However, it was in the treatment of the test conditions for our synaesthetes that we were most demanding. I will cover these changes in some detail later in this chapter, but before giving a specific example of experimental design issues, let's consider these issues in theoretical terms.

Scientific method

A popular first year undergraduate essay topic for psychologists is to discuss psychology's status as a science. Psychology is often regarded as a 'soft' science, in common with sociology and in comparison with 'hard' sciences like chemistry, biology, and physics. To my way of thinking, trying to show that one science is harder than another is quite a challenge. Is, for example, chemistry 'harder' than physics? Or biology 'softer' than chemistry and, if it is, how could one justify such a view? My view is that any discipline that adopts scientific methodology justifies the epithet 'science', a definition that puts psychology firmly in the category of sciences. So what do I mean by scientific methodology? Let me explain.

Hypotheses

At the outset of an experiment the scientist is required to have formed an experimental hypothesis that is typically stated as a proposition. These kinds of explanations are always better illustrated by example, so we will take a well-known effect and seek to show how a piece of common sense can be shown to be true scientifically. Let's say that the experiment is designed to show that drinking alcohol slows one's reaction times. In this example our experimental hypothesis (denoted as H_1) is that drinking alcohol will lengthen reaction latency. Having set our H_1 we now need to specify our alternative or null hypothesis (H_0), which in this case would be that alcohol has no effect on reaction time latency. So far so good, we have specified both our experimental and our null hypotheses. We now need to test these mutually exclusive hypotheses; in short, we need a paradigm.

Operationalizing a hypothesis

We now need an effective method for measuring reaction time so that we can determine whether imbibing alcohol slows our speed of response. Computers are a popular platform for conducting this kind of work, so for our experiment we will ask participants to press the space bar on the computer keyboard whenever a red square appears on the computer screen. The computer will then record how quickly after the onset of the 'stimulus' the 'response' was made. To obtain a good estimate of each participant's reaction time speed, the response speed is measured 10 times, after having given each 5 practice trials. The reaction time measurement provides us with what scientists would call a dependent variable. In this example, we believe that reaction time latency is dependent upon alcohol consumption, and alcohol intake is the variable we propose to manipulate. We are free to vary the levels of alcohol administered and so this variable, which lies within our control, is known technically as the independent variable. Consider now how we should best exercise our power over the independent variable to test the two hypotheses.

Between or within?

Essentially there are two ways in which the experiment could be conducted. One method would involve testing participants while free of alcohol and then giving them some alcohol and retesting. Thus the comparison we are making is 'within' the same participants, hence this design is described as a 'within subjects' design. This design is also sometimes referred to as a 'repeated measures' comparison. An alternative to this design is to conduct a 'between subjects' design. In this design two groups of participants are recruited, one of which is given alcohol (the experimental group) and one that is not (the control group). Reaction time latency is measured and the performance of the two groups is compared.

There are pros and cons attached to the use of these two fundamental designs. The biggest issue when using repeated measures designs is that participants' reaction time latencies might improve as a result of practice. Thus, in our experiment any increase in reaction time caused by alcohol consumption might be masked by reductions in reaction latency caused by practice. This practice effect is referred to technically as a 'confounding variable' and also as an 'order effect', as performance in the two experimental conditions (before or after alcohol) is affected by the order in which they are presented.

Counterbalancing

A popular method of controlling order effects is to counterbalance the experiment. To control for the possibility of order effects in our experiment we would need to test half of our participants sober and then under the influence and the other half first under the influence and then a second time when sober. The first counterbalance condition of sober then drunk is relatively easy to do, probably taking 30 minutes or so, as it takes about 20 minutes for the effect of alcohol consumption to be felt. However, counterbalance condition two could take quite a bit longer, as it would take

30 minutes to put our participants 'under the influence' and then quite a lot longer for them to sober up to complete the second reaction time condition. A between subjects comparison offers an advantage here as, with two groups, we would not need to wait for participants to sober up before they could be retested. Most disciplines that use the scientific method tend to adopt between rather than within comparisons. However, scientists who have people rather than particles or chemicals as the focus of their study often prefer to use repeated measures designs. The reason for this is simple; people vary a great deal, both in their physical make-up and their behaviour. Examples pertinent to our alcohol and reaction time experiment would include factors such as the speed with which different individuals absorb and metabolize alcohol. This turns out to be a good example, as considerable variation exists with regard to the capacity of different ethnic groups to metabolize alcohol. A large proportion of individuals from Asian populations are deficient in the enzyme aldehyde dehydrogenase. This deficiency slows the rate at which alcohol is metabolized, leading to prolonged intoxication. Individuals within any sample selected would probably vary with regard to their ability to metabolize alcohol.

Differential rate of alcohol metabolism is an example of a confounding variable with obvious physiological origins. However, people are just as psychologically complex as they are physically variable. For example, participants in reaction time experiments will vary substantially with regard to the speed at which they will 'naturally' respond. Some individuals will approach the experiment with considerable caution, thereby making few errors but performing at very modest speeds. If, by chance, we ended up with more cautious responders in this group then this would potentially confound our results. Others will be more *laissez-faire* and will sacrifice accuracy to speed their responses. Performance can be made more uniform through the delivery of specific instructions, such as 'I would like you to go as fast as possible, but without making too many errors'. This does not ensure that all participants adopt the same criteria, but it does help to control the experiment.

The drawback to using between groups comparisons is that, when using this design, it is necessary to match the two groups as closely as possible. Most experimenters would match the groups for at least age and sex, while others will have whole lists of variables upon which the experimental groups should be matched.

Comparing performance

So, to recap, we are going to adopt a between groups design and test the reaction time of group 1, who are given 2 pints of alcohol-free beer, and group 2, who will be given 2 points of real beer. Why give group 1 anything at all? Why not just give them nothing to drink or a glass of water? Essentially because, as we have already seen, people are complex organisms. A further manifestation of this complexity is the tendency for people to get better or worse because they expect to do so. This placebo (Latin for 'I shall please') effect is well known in medicine; many patients have been seen to improve as the result of receiving an inert drug that they believe is the real thing. Giving group 2 beer might induce them to do worse because they expect to perform less well. By giving group 1 alcohol-free beer we can look to see whether any observed differences in reaction time latency are due to placebo rather than alcohol. Finally, we have the chance to compare the performance of the two groups, which we shall do using statistics, but not just the descriptive statistics discussed above and in Chapter 3. To test our experimental hypothesis thoroughly we shall need to use inferential statistics.

Applying research methods to the study group

In addition to testing our synaesthete group, we also tested a group of non-synaesthetes. These individuals were designed to be the control group for the study, and were matched with the synaesthetic group for age, sex, IQ, verbal memory, and visual memory. This precaution meant that, for all these variables, the two groups were as similar as possible. This way the results of the study could more certainly be attributed to the presence of synaesthesia, rather than a difference in the intelligence or cognitive abilities of our synaesthetes. We also made the test condition more difficult for the synaesthetes than for the control participants. The two groups were both tested twice with the new test of genuineness and on both occasions their responses were noted. Treatment of the two groups varied on a number of dimensions:

- The control group was retested just 1 week after the first test, whereas we waited for more than 1 year to retest our synaesthetes.

- Control participants were informed that they would be retested on their colour associations 1 week after the first test. In contrast, the synaesthetes were not advised that they would be retested.

- Controls were also encouraged to devise effective strategies for trying to remember the colour–word associations they generated and were requested to adopt mnemonic techniques to aid them. The members of the synaesthete group were not encouraged to use strategies.

Once the results of this testing had been collated, we submitted the test and retest colour associations and correspondences to three judges, who were all asked to determine independently how similar the two colour descriptions seemed to be. These judges were given training for this task and as a result we found that they agreed perfectly with one another in 93% of all cases.

And the winner is...

The results of our study were overwhelming. The control participants were able to keep an average 37% of their test and retest descriptions sufficiently similar to pass the scrutiny of our three judges, whereas the average performance of the synaesthetic group was better than 92%. This result was clearly and overwhelmingly significant, but the question for scientists is always whether the results are statistically significant or not. In this next section I will describe how this is determined.

Group statistical analysis

As discussed in Chapter 2, the classical literature is almost entirely based on narrative accounts of single case studies of individuals with synaesthesia. In rare instances there are published accounts of synaesthetes whose data is reported using descriptive statistics. This form of reporting involves manipulating the data so that 'average' performance can be reported, together with some measures of the distribution of the data around that average. In Chapter 3 reference was made to the calculation of means and standard deviations and how they can be used to determine whether an individual's performance is within or without the normal range. In this chapter these notions are developed to include an account of how the same statistical principles can be used to test scientific theory.

There are three kinds of lies: lies, damned lies, and statistics

You may concur with Benjamin Disraeli's admonition. Personally, I don't; however, what is true is that it is possible to hoodwink statistically naïve individuals. Whatever the case, we need to call upon statistical techniques as scientists. So, let us refresh ourselves with a second cup of tea with Sir Ronald Fisher. The enquiry was how likely was it that Ms Bristol could correctly determine milk or tea first on six out of eight occasions. Sir Ronald calculated that the probability of this occurring just by chance was about one in four, too slim to conclude that she could really tell milk first or milk second. So, at what point do we accept that there is a real effect and that our results are not just due to chance? Any experimental outcome could of course occur just by chance; this is why we can never prove our theories are true, because no matter how unlikely it is that the outcome could have occurred by chance, we can never be sure that our real effect is true. All well and good, but we have to base decisions upon our experimental findings, drugs have to be considered for approval, crops evaluated for their grain yield, etc., and so we need a level of probability to be set so that outcomes less likely than this level can be determined to be because of a real effect. By convention this level is set at 0.05 or 5%; in other words, if the results of our study had a less than 1 in 20 probability of occurring by chance then it is accepted that they are due to a real effect. So, why 5%? A good question. Probably apocryphal stories told me by statisticians suggest that Sir Ronald Fisher (him again) was contemplating this issue in the bath one day. Whilst in the course of this contemplation he fixed his gaze on one of his feet. On seeing five toes Sir Ronald peremptorily determined that the 5% level was appropriate (this may or may not be true, but I am in any case grateful to Dr Ken McRae for the story).

Now what are the chances of that happening?

So, what of the relative performance of our putative synaesthetes and our control participants? Unsurprisingly, the difference of 37.6% versus 92.3% proved to be highly statistically different. In fact, the probability of this outcome occurring by chance was found to be less than 0.001%. We therefore concluded that our results were due to a real effect and that this effect was most probably synaesthesia. However, it became clear that the correspondences recounted by our synaesthetes appeared to be much less complex than those provided by Elizabeth.

Predictable single colours versus unpredictable complex colours

You will doubtless recall from Chapter 3 that it proved impossible to find a pattern in Elizabeth's colour correspondences? This finding was not reproduced with our group of synaesthetes, as it emerged from further analysis that their word–colour correspondences were based on the dominant letter, or letters, of the word. Thus if M was red, then the chances are that moon, mouse, meteor, etc. would all be red in colour. This difference in our findings prompted us to wonder whether other facets of Elizabeth's experience of the condition were shared by our new experimental participants. We were therefore particularly pleased to have collected the structured interview data with them, the results of which are now recounted.

A return to introspection

Having testable hypotheses is all very well, but most students of human behaviour would have to admit occasionally to having their thoughts driven by data. Sometimes when an experiment has been completed, it is possible to have a bit of fun with the dataset and look to see if there is anything interesting. So commonplace is this desire that psychologists have borrowed a statistical technique (factor analysis) to assist them in these trawls through the data. These analyses are sometimes referred to as 'unplanned comparisons' to differentiate them from the formal tests of our experimental hypothesis, which is referred to as 'planned comparison'.

An experimental method popular in the late nineteenth century was a technique described as introspection. As the name suggests, this technique relied upon asking the participant to describe a perceptual or cognitive event. So, for example, in a bid to understand the perceptual processes underlying colour, participants would be asked to imagine pure red and then describe the experience to the experimenter. It is probably quite hard to explain what a pure experience of red would be like, largely because our experience of colour is in the context of its form, e.g. a red card or a red balloon. Nevertheless, in the absence of anything better, introspection proved a popular method for exploring subjective experience. Introspection was one of the first major casualties of behaviourism and was so vilified that as a technique it has never recovered its former respectability. Many contemporary psychologists lament the loss of this tool from the already modest shed of psychological techniques. I would count myself amongst them and, when faced with a condition such as synaesthesia, it seems to me that it is only sensible to listen and report what those with the condition are telling us. In our group study of synaesthetes we were keen to let them tell us about their experience so that we could make comparisons between them. We had expected some similarity in the accounts they gave us, but we had no expectation that these accounts would be quite so similar. What further fascinated us was the similarity between what our contemporary synaesthetes told us and the accounts of synaesthesia written a hundred years ago.

When does synaesthesia begin?

It is our universal experience that individuals with synaesthesia report having had the condition for as long as they can remember. This was found to be true of not just our sample of seven synaesthetes, but of the entire 212 who responded to Baron-Cohen's questionnaire. This finding is also found in reports from the end of the nineteenth century. Starr, for example, writing in 1893, recounts that her synaesthetic participant GL recalled having synaesthesia from 'early childhood'. We have made the assumption that synaesthesia is a lifelong condition and its presence in early childhood fits well with our theory of the cause of the condition. When we first began interviewing people with synaesthesia is was tempting to ask whether they liked having the condition. This was a naïve question on our part – how could they know otherwise? Their replies to this question almost universally confirmed that they were pleased to have synaes-thesia but that a judgement was hard to make because they had never known what it was like not to have the condition. In fact, the childhood assumption made by almost every synaes-thete we have met is that everyone has the condition. They have often been very surprised to find that this was not the case. Richard Cytowic makes the same observation, noting that 'synaesthetes often say that their gift has existed as far back as they can remember and are surprised to discover that others do not perceive the world as they do'. This same per-spective also features in the older literature. Isador Coriat noted, in a description of a 35-year-old female synaesthete in 1913, that 'as with most subjects afflicted with coloured hear-ing, up to the age of fourteen or fifteen she did not have the slightest doubt but that everyone experienced a sensation of colour on hearing a spoken word'.

The discovery that not everyone sees colours when they hear words is generally made in childhood or adolescence and often leads to synaesthetes becoming tight-lipped about their gift. Every synaesthete we have met can recall the occasion when they learnt that their condition was not commonplace. A typical anecdote given by one of the seven individuals reported in our 1993 study serves to illustrate this well:

> I remember coming home from school as a relatively young child, perhaps aged about 7 or 8 years, and commenting to my mother that our teacher's name, Mr Brown, was peculiar because his name was green. My mother became quite concerned at this and responded to my comment in such a way as to persuade me that I should never again offer this kind of comment.

Again, this kind of comment is a frequent feature of the classic literature, with commentators such as Starr recording that the participant GL, mentioned in Chapter 2, 'when a very little girl was laughed at because she said that names were coloured'.

This reluctance to share their experience is interesting in the context of the accusation that claiming synaesthesia is just attention-seeking behaviour. I mention this because a common point of view amongst some audience members at talks I have given on synaesthesia is that the motivation for people to say they have the condition is an attempt to draw attention to themselves. This may be true of some, or perhaps even the majority of the individuals we have encountered. However, such a view sits very ill indeed with the data we have, which suggests that, in the vast majority of cases, synaesthetes have remained silent about their gift for virtually the whole of their lives.

'Where' is the synaesthesic percept and what does it look like?

Before we tackle this let me offer a note of caution to all non-synaesthetes reading this book. After more than ten years of reading about the condition and talking to those who have it, I am no nearer to genuine understanding either of what it is like to have synaesthesia or what synaesthetes 'see' when they hear words. However, let me become a little introspective in a bid to help non-synaesthetes out. My experience of 'seeing things' can be divided into three 'types' of event.

1. Visual information received by my eyes
The human visual system is fairly well mapped in terms of its anatomy and physiology. I, like the majority of my species, have specialist cells in my retina (rods and cones)

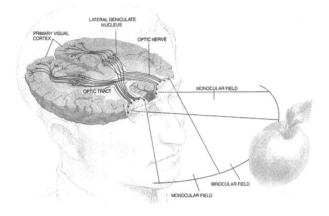

Figure 11 Visual pathway in the adult demonstrates the segregation of axons. The axons corresponding to the right eye are in red, and those corresponding to the left eye are in blue. Neighbouring retinal ganglion cells in each eye send their axons to neighbouring neurons in the lateral geniculate nucleus. Similarly, the neurons of the geniculate nucleus map their axons onto the visual cortex. The system forms a topographically orderly pattern that in part accounts for such characteristics as binocular vision. See also Plate 2.

which are stimulated by light. The cone system allows day vision and the rod system gives a much poorer quality night vision. As can be seen from Figure 11, the information is received by cells in the retina and is then relayed to the visual parts of the brain in the occipital lobes, via the lateral geniculate nuclei of the thalamus, the so-called telephone exchange of the brain.

In the occipital lobes this information is processed by specialist areas dealing with colour, form, and motion. Somehow this information is put together to form an assembled image. I'd like to explain how this happens – but we don't know. It is at this point, as the physiologist Sir Charles Sherrington* poetically commented, 'that the scheme places its finger to its lips and is silent'. This 'binding problem', as it has come to be known, remains one of the most critical outstanding questions to be solved by neuroscience.

2. Images conjured up at will and seen in my mind's eye

This form of visual experience is what in folk psychological terms we would describe as imagining a visual event. The subjective experience of this type of seeing is a bit like having a cinema screen in your head – you think of the object or scene you wish to view and it is there in your mind's eye. Two quick observations about the mind's eye. First, it seems that the ability is not universal; many individuals claim not to have the ability to see things with the mind's eye. The second is that we are not entirely clear how or what these mental pictures are. I remember discussing this issue with Professor Leslie Henderson, my PhD supervisor, when he asked me to conduct a thought experiment. He first asked me if I was familiar with the British Museum, which I

---

* Sherrington's prose style is such a pleasure to read. The quotation cited above is merely one of a selection of exquisitely worded descriptions. Sherrington is equally eloquent in his description of the developing brain. Enjoy this wonderful example:
'Swiftly the head-mass becomes an enchanted loom where millions of flashing shuttles weave a dissolving pattern, always a meaningful pattern though never an abiding one, a shifting harmony of subpatterns'.

confirmed I was. He then invited me to envisage the building in my mind's eye, which I did. At his further invitation I
then described the image, providing a passingly good
description of the building. He then asked me the critical
question: 'How many columns support the pediment over
the main entrance?' I guessed six (there are in fact eight),
but immediately acknowledged his point. I felt I could see
it, but I couldn't use the image to answer simple questions
about one of the building's most prominent features
correctly.

3. Things I think I am seeing but which I know are not 'out there', i.e. not part of the world

As a young boy I was once in the grip of a febrile illness that
required me to have antibiotics. As a consequence of taking
these drugs, or of the fever, I complained to my parents that
I had unexpected company. Apparently, polar bears were
now freely wandering my room. Needless to say these particular bears were 'phantoms of the mind', the only hallucinations I ever recall experiencing. Also, I very occasionally
experience visual events when waking from a dream. The
objects that I believe I am seeing often seem related to the
dream from which I am waking. Such experiences are, I
am assured, quite commonplace, and are described as
hypnopompic imagery. Other people, it seems, also experience such events when on the cusp of sleep, so-called hypnagogic images. I very rarely experience these images, but
when it happens the effect is very strong; my perception is
that the image is very real. The nature of the experience,
though in this case as an auditory hallucination, is for me
exquisitely described by Keats in the excellent *Ode to a
Nightingale*, in which he fancies he is listening to a nightingale sing but is left wondering:

Was it a vision, or a waking dream?
Fled is that music – Do I wake or sleep?

This perfectly characterizes my uncertainty of hypno-pompia. It is only moments later, when fully awake, that I am able to rationalize the event and conclude that Victoria Principal and Debbie Harry were unlikely ever to have been in my bedroom.

These are all areas of vision shared with the synaesthetes I have met over the years and, at the beginning of our studies of the condition, appeared to provide a reference by which one might be able to imagine what the experience of synaesthesia is like. However, every synaesthete I have met assures me that their experience is not 'out there'. By this they mean that the experience of colour perceived on hearing sound does not colour the outside world. So, synaesthesia does not appear to be confused with visual stimuli received by the eye. In fact, synaesthetes are very specific on this; there is a clear difference between visual stimulation received by the eye and that stimulated by sound.

Synaesthetes are equally clear that the perceptual experience they have is not seen in the mind's eye. The synaesthetes to whom we have asked this question understand precisely what creating these images is like and are certain that their synaesthesia is categorically not like imagined objects and scenes. So, what of our final category, things we see but know are not there? Interestingly, this category of events shares something in common with the hallucinatory experiences I have described; specifically, that although they 'see' the percept they know it is not part of the outside world. Is a visual synaesthesia 'like' a hallucination? Well, not really, it seems. The few synaesthetes that we have inter-viewed who also experience hypnopompia and hypnagogia assure us that their synaesthesia is not like this. One synaes-thete mentioned that she often 'saw stars' when rising too quickly from a seated position, but that this was also unlike the synaesthetic experience.

This leaves we non-synaesthetes in ignorance. If their experience isn't like retinal vision, imagined pictures or hal-lucination, what is it like? Truthfully, I have no idea, but I do have a yet untested hypothesis that might help us, the unblessed, to understand what it is to have synaesthesia, and it is perhaps something like dream images.

Dreams and other forms of direct occipital stimulation

Why do we dream and what do dreams mean, if anything? Theories vary, 'dreaming helps us to make sense of the day's activities', 'dreams are opportunities for the subconscious to tell us what we're *really* thinking', etc. Another theory holds that dreams are important in our early development, an observation that is proffered as an explanation for why neonates (babies) sleep longer and spend more time in dream sleep than adults. An unfashionable, but possibly accurate, view of dreams is that they have no purpose. This seems hard for us to believe, driven, as we appear to be, to find reasons for everything we experience. Nevertheless, the compulsion to believe that dreams have a purpose is strong. I agree that, from a subjective point of view, dreams can have the potency of real experience, hence Keats' confusion about the nightingale's song. Our experience of dreams is that they have a narrative style that implies meaning, no matter how bizarre that narrative might be. The work of Salvador Dali stands as excellent testimony to this. So, what do we know of the physiology of sleep and can this knowledge help us to understand the nature of synaesthesia? I believe it can, so here is my theory of dreaming and how it can help us with synaesthesia.

Sources of 'visual' stimulation

Our day-to-day conscious experience of vision is based on light travelling from the retina as electrochemical events, through the LGN (lateral geniculate nucleus), to the occipital lobes where it is turned into visual interpretations of the outside world. However, it is also possible for electrical stimulation from brain locations other than the retina to arrive at the LGN and thence to the occipital lobes. This is what appears to happen during dream sleep. In the case of dreaming, electrochemical stimulation originates not from the retina but from a brainstem region deep within the brain called the pons (Latin for bridge). During dream sleep bursts of electrical activity originating in the pons travel through the LGN and on to the visual cortex. The visual cortex does not know that these PGO (pons–geniculate–occipital) spikes are not from the retina and so processes these spikes as it would any other incoming activity. Just as the brain seeks to impose meaning on retinally derived stimuli (think of the dog, and the horse and rider images in Chapter 2), so it tries to interpret these pons generated signals meaningfully. Thus these meaningless PGO spikes are constructed as meaningful images, even though successive constructs may be unconnected. Dream images, according to this very unoriginal hypothesis, are the visual cortices' interpretation of essentially random bursts of electrical impulses originating in the pons. When we awake with the most recent constructs still in our consciousness, we put these images together into a narrative. Nice theory, you may be thinking, but how does this help with synaes-thesia? Well, the theory helps in that it reminds us that what our brains 'see' is not always derived from what hits the reti-na, suggesting that if we stimulated the appropriate part of the visual cortex we could create colour images. How would we do this? Well, actually it has already been done, as we shall see.

Wilder Penfield's experimental neurosurgery

The brain feels no pain, which, as well as being a poor rhyme, also means that some forms of neurosurgery can be conducted under local rather than general anaesthesia. Put yourself in the surgical boots of the Canadian neurosurgeon Wilder Penfield. You've got the top of your patient's skull off and the operation is completed – how can you kill a bit of time? Why not stimulate the surface of their brain elec-trically and see what happens? Which is precisely what he did.

Penfield discovered that when he stimulated a strip of the frontal lobe that we now call the motor projection area, the patient experienced the movement of body parts but denied any intention to move. To generate the movement it would be necessary to stimulate the left frontal lobe at a point towards the top of the motor projection area. What hap-pened when the visual areas were stimulated? Typically patients reported vivid optical experiences such as flicker-ing lights and formless colours. This is another form of non-retinal stimulation of the visual cortices, but this time yielding formless colours that defy perfect description – does this sound familiar?

The obvious experiment to do is to open up the cranium of some individuals with synaesthesia, directly stimulate their visual cortex and see if the resulting experience is similar to their experience of synaesthesia. Scientifically fascinating, but ethically dubious you're thinking? True, but recent developments in the techniques available to neuroscience provide us with an alternative, considerably more benign method of directly stimulating the visual cortex which is gloriously named transcranial magnetic stimulation, or TMS for short.

Hit me baby, one more time

So, how does TMS work? The basis of the technology is the generation of a magnetic pulse which passes through the skull and causes nerve cells in the brain to fire. It sounds horrendous but other than the sharp, but surprisingly quiet 'zap', the technique seems perfectly safe. TMS has proven popular among physiologists, and has found interesting and useful applications in neuroscience. One TMS experiment, cited by Zeki, was conducted by Becker and Becker, who magnetically stimulated the occipital lobes and found that it was possible to elicit colour percepts. These 'chromatophenes', as the Beckers called them, were reported by participants as being clearly coloured and of a form best described as oval. This is not quite the apparently pure experience of colour reported by some of Penfield's neurosurgical patients. However, the magnetic pulse delivered using TMS is much less spatially precise than the application of an electrical stimulator used by Penfield. The brain regions serving colour and form are relatively close by, and so it is difficult to stimulate specific visual regions selectively. An experiment that might prove rewarding would involve stimulating the same brain regions in synaesthetes as in the participants tested by Becker and Becker. These synaesthetic participants would then be able to compare the elicited chromatophenes with their synaesthesic percepts and report how similar the two 'visual' events are. If they turn out to be similar we might, all of us, discover what it is like to have synaesthesia.

This last section has identified that, due to electrochemical nerve impulses from non-retinal brain areas, we can 'see' far more than comes through our retinae. This general notion plays a key role in the theory about the causes of synaesthesia, a theory described in Chapter 1, which holds that synaesthesia is because of auditory electrical impulses stimulating visual areas.

Was it in black and white, or colour?

The discussion of dream images provides me with a neat lead into one of the other consistent characteristics of the synaesthetes we have interviewed and tested. However, before we discuss the details of the issue that we have sought to answer, take a moment to reflect on this question – do you dream in colour? It has long fascinated me that, according to the literature on dreaming, most people report that they dream in black and white. Even more fascinating is the experience of a number of individuals that they do not recollect ever having dreamed at all. For my own part, I can readily confirm that I do dream and that most often I am aware that my dreams are in colour. This response is typically always the response of people with synaesthesia. What is also remarkable about their response is the immediacy and conviction of their reply. They typically answer straight away that they indeed dream in colour. My experience of asking non-synaesthetes is that they have to spend some time thinking about the question before deciding one way or the other. So, a further shared and consistent characteristic of people with synaesthesia is that they *know* they dream in colour. It is hard to know what we should make of this, if anything, but it is worth reminding you that the New York painter studied by Oliver Sacks and reported in Chapter 3, lost his colour vision, his synaesthesia, and his ability to dream in colour as a consequence of his brain injury. Perhaps the colour component of all three of these abilities shares a common neural substrate? Food for thought.

Let's now leave our consideration of dreams and percepts to continue with our consideration of the questionnaire data collected for the 1993 paper.

Do synaesthetes all see the same word–colour correspondences?

It is clear from the historical literature that for two synaesthetes to have the same colour–word correspondences would be extraordinarily rare. We have never found so much as mild similarity in the correspondences reported by different synaesthetes, even in the few cases we have encountered where identical twins both have the condition. However, while no two synaesthetes appear to see the same colour for any particular word, the word–colour association for any individual synaesthete remains invariant across a lifetime, which is a good job, as the test of genuineness depends on this being the case! It is apparently as Galton proclaimed, 'that no two people agree, or hardly ever do so, as to the colour they associate with the same sound'.

Attention to detail

Galton also noted that the descriptions given of synaesthesic percepts were very exact, specifically that:

> seers are invariably most minute in their description of the
> precise tint and hue of the colour. They are never satisfied,
> for instance, with saying 'blue', but will take a great deal of
> trouble to express or to match the particular blue they mean.

This observation again very much mirrors our synaesthetes' experience of providing colour descriptions. In the
1987 study of Elizabeth's synaesthesia, verbal descriptions
were noted for each word. In the 1993 study we sought to
control the recording of colour correspondences better
by using a standard paint chart matrix of more than
250 colours. However, from the very outset of this study it
was clear that participants were dissatisfied at the selection
offered, usually making do by picking a colour swatch that
represented the colour closest to that of their synaesthesic
percept.

It's a family affair

A final, consistent, characteristic of the synaesthetes interviewed for the 1993 paper was their preparedness to tell us
of other family members that they knew to have the condition. In almost all cases, exclusively female relatives were
reported. This was entirely consistent with the responses
provided in answer to the same question in the questionnaire study. These remarkable results suggest that the vast
majority of synaesthetes are females, with only a small
minority of men amongst them. This effect prompted us
to adopt a further line of investigation – specifically to
determine the frequency with which synaesthesia occurs

in the general population, the extent to which it runs in families, and, most importantly, to explore whether there may be a genetic basis to the condition. More on this in Chapter 8.

Figure 12 Charles Baudelaire. Photograph by Carjat (Mary Evans Picture Library)

CHAPTER 5

When is synaesthesia not synaesthesia? When it is a metaphor

There's something you may have noticed about people with synaesthesia, i.e. they tend to be women? What is immediately curious about the figures from history who, it is claimed, are or were synaesthetes is the overwhelming preponderance of males. Before we proceed it is again time for a little honesty. What is clear from the foregoing chapters is that there are objective means of determining whether any given individual has synaesthesia. However, we have no 'dead tissue' method of determining this and consequently no method of confirming or denying whether any now dead figure was indeed a synaesthete. One day, assuming we obtain a dead tissue technique for diagnosing synaesthesia, we might read about the work of a scientist who has managed to obtain remains of long dead 'synaesthetes' to verify which of them really had the condition. However, as of now we have neither the remains nor the technique. But let us indulge our fancy and assume that a foolproof dead tissue technique exists – who would we recommend for exhumation?

The usual suspects

Who usually goes into the line-up? Well, mostly a succession of individuals from the end of the nineteenth century and early part of the twentieth century. Let's have a stroll down the line and see if there is anyone we can pick out.

Charles Baudelaire (1821–1867)

Charles Baudelaire, the poet, essayist, and salon art critic, appears to have believed in the unity of sensation. His poem *Correspondances* suggests a link between sound and colour, as illustrated in the second stanza of this piece:

> Comme de longs échos qui de loin se confondent
> *Like long echoes which from a distance mingle*
> Dans une ténébreuse et profonde unité
> *Into a shadowy and deep unity*
> Vaste comme la nuit et comme la clarté
> *As vast as night and light*
> Les parfums, les couleurs et les sons se répondent
> *Perfumes, colours and sounds reply to one another*

Elsewhere Baudelaire informs us that his synaesthesia 'assumes an unaccustomed vividness' during his use of hashish, a substance which he used in large doses over a protracted period of time. He also writes that hashish has the effect of enhancing the synaesthetic experience, implying that Baudelaire at least believed himself to be a synaesthete, consistent with his assertion in 1857 that 'sounds are clad in colour'. The question to which we must find a satisfactory answer is how good a witness Baudelaire was to his own subjective experience. A standard experimental precaution adopted by psychologists is to screen out participants who may confound interpretation. For example,

there is considerable evidence that the cognitive performance of individuals with schizophrenia is deficient. Consequently, these individuals make poor study participants
for neuropsychologists, who tend to be interested in the
impact of circumscribed brain lesions of the kind discussed
in Chapter 3. The challenge is always to show unequivocally that any cognitive deficit is due to a specific brain lesion.
An obvious alternative explanation for cognitive deficits
seen in patients with schizophrenia is the very presence of
the disease itself. Susan Greenfield has recently commented
that patients with schizophrenia have been reported to
experience synaesthesia. However, this poses science a
problem. Many individuals with schizophrenia also report
hearing voices. We, the impartial observers, do not believe
that these voices are in any sense real, just as we doubt these
patients' accounts of visual hallucinations. It could be that
synaesthesia is part of the disease, or diseases, that constitute schizophrenia. Unfortunately, it is sometimes hard
to accept at face value the experiences reported by those
suffering from psychosis.

So, what reasons could we have for distrusting Baudelaire's
synaesthesia? Although we have no evidence of the presence
of psychosis, we do know that for much of his life
Baudelaire suffered from syphilis, a disease that in the later
stages can attack the brain. We also know that a number of
psychoactive substances can give rise to synaesthesia. In
fact, a contemporary of Baudelaire's, the French scientist
Gautier, reported in 1843 that he had been able to produce
'pseudo sensations of colour' artificially, in particular by the
use of hashish. Other drugs, such as LSD, mescaline (from
the Mexican peyote cactus) and psilocybin (mostly derived
from the fungi of the psilocybe family, so-called 'magic
mushrooms'), have all been reported to cause confusion

between the sensory modalities. In some cases, use of these hallucinogens has caused sounds to be perceived as visions.

Arthur Rimbaud (1854–1891)

A second nineteenth century French poet, Arthur Rimbaud, also made a link between sound and colour in his *Le sonnet des voyelles*, which begins:

> A black, *E* white, *I* red, *U* green, *O* blue;
> Some day I'll crack your nascent origins.

This is apparently good evidence for a synaesthetic link, but consider the rest of of the poem:

> A Hairy corset of clacking black flies
> Bombarding agony pits of stench-ridden darkness;
> *E* Frankness in steamers and pavilions, lances
> Of lofty glaciers, white kings, shivering umbrels.

Rich pictures to illustrate the colour associations drawn by Rimbaud, but it is not clear that this is sound evidence in support of his status as a synaesthete. Lawrence Marks, writing in 1975, reminds us that Rimbaud later remarked that these vowel–colour associations were his invention, literally 'J'inventais la couler des voyelles!'

Joris-Karl Huysmans (1848–1907)

It seems certain that Huysmans was very well acquainted with the work of the two aforementioned French symbolist poets. As with both Rimbaud and Baudelaire, there is no autobiographical evidence in support of Huysmans having synaesthesia. The assertion seems to originate as the result of a number of commentators describing the anti-hero of Huysmans' decadent *fin de siécle* novel *Against Nature*, as being 'Huysmans himself in the thinnest of disguises'. As Huysmans imbued his hero, Duc Jean Floressas des Esseintes,

Jorris Karl Huysmans, † am 12. Mai.

with a form of taste–sound synaesthesia it seemed at least possible that Huysmans himself may have been a synaesthete. *Against Nature* remains my favourite novel and is, as Oscar Wilde writes for the character of Dorian Gray:

> The strangest book that he had ever read. It seemed to him that in exquisite raiment and to the delicate sound of flutes, the sins of the world were passing a dumb show before him. Things that he had dimly dreamed of were suddenly made real to him. Things of which he had never dreamed were gradually revealed.

Amongst these 'sins of the world' were curious sexual peccadillos involving ventriloquist prostitutes, cuisine based on texture and ingested by suppository, and a curious evening spent creating alcoholic symphonies with his collection of liqueurs:

> Each and every liqueur, in his opinion, corresponded in taste to the sound of a particular instrument. Dry curaçao, for instance, was like the clarinet with its piercing, velvety note; kümmel like the oboe with its sonorous, nasal timbre; crème de menthe and anisette like the flute, at once sweet and tart, soft, and shrill. To complete the orchestra there was kirsch, blowing a wild trumpet blast; gin and whisky raising the roof of the mouth with the blare of their cornets and trombones; marc-brandy matching the tubas with its deafening din; while peals of thunder came from the cymbal and the bass drum, which arak and mastic were banging and beating with all their might.

Alexander Scriabin (1872–1915)

Towards the end of Des Esseintes' liqueur-induced musical evening he speculates 'that Benedictine represents, so to speak, the minor key corresponding to the major key of those alcohols which wine-merchants' scores indicate by the name of green chartreuse'. We are not informed which

key this 'work' is to be played in, but the notion that musical keys can be represented in senses other than sound is clearly implied, however playfully. In the cases of two famous Russian composers, it would seem that they most earnestly believed that musical keys possessed specific colour qualities. It seems that these two individuals, Alexander Scriabin and Nicholas Rimsky-Korsakov, seldom agreed on colour–key associations, as shown by the few examples listed in the following Table.

Key	Scriabin	Rimsky-Korsakov
C major	Red	White
D major	Yellow	Yellow
E flat major	Steely	Dark bluish-grey
E major	Bluish-white	Sparkling sapphire
F major	Deep red	Green
G major	Orange-rose	Rich gold
A major	Green	Rosy coloured
B flat major	Steely	None attributed

Again, the issue here would appear to be whether these associations are metaphoric or genuinely synaesthetic. Colour and music have been associated ever since classical times. A number of famous figures have sought to find links between the two. Sir Isaac Newton (1642–1727), for example, was struck by the fact that there are seven primary colours in the spectrum and seven notes in a scale and tried, unsuccessfully, to find a mathematical method for translating colour to music. A century later Goethe sought to do much the same and extended the notion to include other senses.

Linking colour to music seems to be a very commonplace activity, one I engage in myself. For me Dvorak's 'New World'

Figure 15 Aleksandr Scriabin. Unattributed (1914) (Mary Evans Picture Library)

symphony is a bright pastoral green, the third movement of Beethoven's 5th symphony is black and the fourth movement a bright gold. Equally, Wagner's Pilgrims chorus from *Tannhauser* is a bright blue and Beethoven's moonlight sonata a silvery-blue. However, I am no synaesthete and it seems relatively easy to rationalize the associations listed above. For example, that the moonlight sonata should be silvery-blue is to me a clear association between the title of the music and moonlight colours. I am informed by friends more musical than myself that the moonlight sonata was composed in C sharp minor. However, no other musical works composed in this key have a silvery-blue association for me.

A cursory examination of the literature on Scriabin suggests that the main reason for his association with synaesthesia is the symphonic piece *Prometheus: the poem of fire*, which he composed between 1908 and 1910. *Prometheus* is remarkable for the composer's inclusion of notation for a 'colour organ'. The keys of the clavier a luce, when struck, projected coloured light instead of producing a sound. Myers reports that Scriabin planned to score an orchestral piece, *Mystery*, to include the same colour dimension but this time with the addition of odours.

As I warned at the beginning of this chapter, evidence of synaesthesia in deceased historical figures is remarkably hard to find. The best we can achieve is to establish whether the accounts of the experience given by these individuals are consistent with the accounts given by contemporary synaesthetes. However, we often only have snippets of information, usually little more than interpretations made by others of the individual's use of metaphor. Rarely do we have interview data collected by psychologists of the kind reported in Chapter 4. Fortunately, in the case of Scriabin we have a published account of his synaesthesia in a paper modestly entitled *Two cases of synaesthesia* by an English psychologist named Charles S. Myers.

Myers met Scriabin during a trip made to London by the composer. As Myers spoke no Russian and Scriabin very little English, the conversation was conducted in French. According to Myers' report, Scriabin first became aware of his coloured hearing whilst attending a concert in Paris with his compatriot Rimsky-Korsakov. Scriabin reports commenting to Rimsky-Korsakov that the piece they were listening to seemed to him to be yellow. Rimsky-Korsakov apparently responded that to him the piece was golden, consistent with his colour association for the key D major. Scriabin was apparently well into adulthood at the time of the Parisian concert, an untypically late stage of life for a genuine synaesthete to become aware of their condition. Recall that every verified instance of synaesthesia we have tested has been aware of their synaesthesia for their entire lives. Cytowic implies the same for all 42 of his synaesthetic participants. Myers asked Scriabin about the experience of synaesthesia, just as we asked our synaesthetes more than 70 years later. Scriabin's response to this question is atypical:

> In general, when listening to music, he (Scriabin) has only a 'feeling' of colour; only in cases where the feeling is very intense does it pass over to give an 'image' of colour.

This description stands in marked contrast to the experience of the synaesthetes we have tested. To a person they have stated that the synaesthesic percept is an immediate, irrepressible, and consistent experience. These contemporary accounts also stand at odds with a later comment made by Scriabin that: 'certain compositions, and most of Beethoven's symphonies, are not of a kind to need colour'.

So far, then, the evidence would seem to suggest that Scriabin did not have synaesthesia, in spite of a number of commentators suggesting that his musical key–colour correspondences imply he was the genuine article. However, closer inspection of the evidence adduced by Myers shows that Scriabin had no colour association for the keys of D flat, A flat, E flat, B flat and F. In answer to this, Scriabin suggested that the colours for these keys may well be extraspectral 'either ultraviolet or infrared'. I regard this curious speculation to be the best evidence we have that Scriabin did not have synaesthesia. In our experience, synaesthetes would simply never say such a thing.

Wassily Kandinsky (1866–1944)

Kandinsky, the father of abstraction, was much impressed by Scriabin's efforts and included in the manifesto for his and Franz Marc's Blue Rider group ('*Der Blau Rieter Almanac*') an appraisal of Scriabin's *Prometheus*, or the *Poem of Fire*. Kandinsky appears to have possessed a certain envy of composition as an art form in that music, while being almost totally abstract, can conjure visual images (cf. Debussy's *Au Claire de Lune*, and Wagner's overture to *Das Rheingold*). A point of great inspiration to Kandinsky appears to have been the abstract colour visions described in the novel *Die Andere Seite* (*The Other Side*) by his colleague in the *Neue Künstlervereinigung* group, Alfred Kubin (1877–1959). Kandinsky's move toward total abstraction in his work seems to have followed from his desire to imbue his work with a synaesthesic quality. His intention was for his work to possess the quality of evoking sounds (*klangen*) in those who viewed his canvasses. This evocation of an auditory dimension to visual representations was a move toward Kandinsky's ultimate aim of creating the

Figure 16 Wassily Kandinsky, Evening Standard Collection (© Hulton Getty)

gesamtkunstwerk (total art work). In seeking to create this *gesamtkunstwerk* Kandinsky's logic was simple; the more senses that could be appealed to with a piece of work, the better the chance of touching the inner spirituality within his audience. Kandinsky, in his written work *On the spiritual in art*, appears to take up Wagner's suggestion that it is possible to touch the inner spirituality through the arts. Nevertheless the evidence suggests that Kandinsky was trying to create a synaesthesic dimension to his work, rather than his art being an expression of his synaesthesia.

Olivier Messaien (1908–1992)

I will close the list of synaesthesic composers with a consideration of the French composer, Olivier Messaien. Messaien provides us with what sounds like a particularly florid description of colour–sound association when he described in 1947 'the gentle cascade of blue–orange chords' in the piano part of the second movement of *Quator pour la fin du temps*. He is later more specific about the nature of his synaesthesia when he states that he sees 'colours which move with the music, and I sense these colours in an extremely vivid manner'. We have no particular evidence one way or the other with respect to Messaien's status as a synaesthete. Messaien's statements are ambiguous, as when he writes in his two volume account of his methods of musical composition that 'I try to convey colours through music; certain combinations of tones and certain sonorities are bound by certain colour combinations and I employ them to this end'.

Vladimir Nabokov (1899–1977)

The author Vladimir Nabokov, interviewed in *The Listener* (1962), recounts his 'rather freakish gift of seeing letters in

Figure 17 Olivier Messaien. Photography by Andreossy (Mary Evans Picture Library)

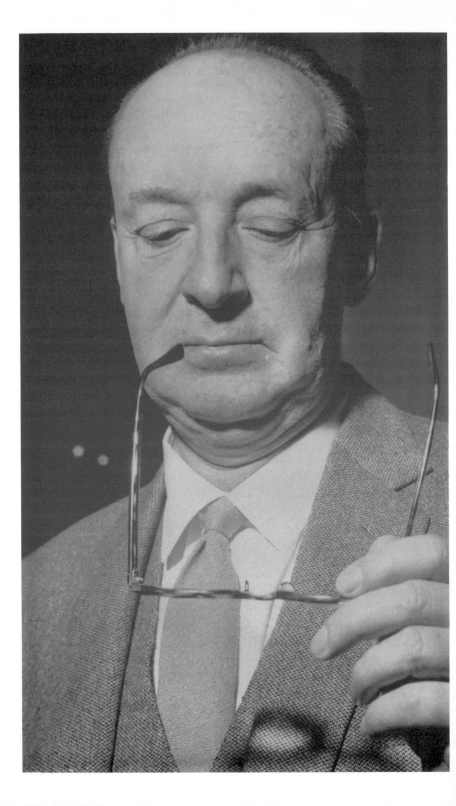

colour'. Interestingly, he states that his wife also has the gift of coloured hearing and that their son sees letters in colour that sometimes appear to be a mix of his parents' colours. For example, for Nabokov the letter M was pink and for his wife, Véra, it was blue. In their son (Dimitri) they found it to be purple, which, as Nabokov suggests, is as if 'genes were painting in aquarelle'. Dimitri Nabokov recently described his synaesthesia in a television documentary by BBC's *Horizon* (December 13th, 1994).

Nabokov writes in considerable detail about both his own and his mother's synaesthesia in his autobiography *Speak, Memory*:

> The confessions of a synesthete must sound tedious and pretentious to those who are protected from such leakings and drafts by more solid walls than mine are. To my mother, though, this all seemed quite normal. The matter came up, one day in my seventh year, as I was using a heap of old alphabet blocks to build a tower. I casually remarked to her that their colours were all wrong.

Nabokov also treats us to a prosaic description of his coloured alphabet:

> I present a fine case of coloured hearing. Perhaps 'hearing' is not quite accurate, since the colour sensation seems to be produced by the very act of my orally forming a given letter while I imagine its outline. The long *a* of the English alphabet (and it is this alphabet I have in mind unless otherwise stated) has for me the tint of weathered wood, but a French *a* evokes polished ebony. This black group also includes hard *g* (vulcanised rubber) and *r* (a sooty rag being ripped). Oatmeal *n*, noodle-limp *l*, and the ivory-backed hand mirror of *o* take care of the whites.

Much of Nabokov's account of his synaesthesia shows a marked similarity to those given by the synaesthetes described in Chapter 4. Participants in our study confirmed

that they too had possessed synaesthesia for as long as they could remember and also reported synaesthesic relatives. Nabokov appears to have been fortunate, compared with many synaesthetes that we have interviewed, in that he recalls revealing his synaesthesia to his mother, who shared the condition.

Sergei Eisenstein (1898–1948)

There is no evidence that Sergei Eisenstein had synaesthesia, though it is sometimes supposed that he did, possibly because of the influence of synaesthesia upon his later work, particularly *Ivan the Terrible: Part 1* and *Part 2: The Boyar's plot*. That synaesthesia should have influenced Eisenstein should come as no surprise; after all, he was a contemporary of Kandinsky and Scriabin. You may also recall from Chapter 3 that Luria's mnemonist and Eisenstein were acquainted – Shereshevski had famously described Eisenstein as having a voice like a flame 'with fibres protruding from it'. Eisenstein's conviction that sound and vision were intimately related may have been further encouraged by his exposure to Japanese *kabuki* theatre. Among his essays on film theory Eisenstein writes about this by way of explanation for his adoption of what he called his 'colour–sound montage'. Eisenstein explains that:

> In experiencing *kabuki* one involuntarily recalls an American novel about a man in whom are transposed the hearing and seeing nerves, so that he perceives light vibrations as sounds and hears tremors of air as colours, he hears *light* and *sees* sound. This is also what happens in *kabuki*.

Elsewhere Eisenstein writes of the relationships between sound and colour, and comments that there is no 'all pervading law of absolute meanings and correspondences between colours and sound'. Synaesthesia, for Eisenstein it would appear, is an influence upon his work, but probably not part of his biological make-up. However, his reference to *kabuki* is interesting, as synaesthesic references appear in many forms of Japanese literature, particularly in *haiku* poems.

Basho Matsuo (1644–1694)

The amount of information that exists with which to *infer* that any of these individuals had synaesthesia varies substantially. In the case of the Japanese *haiku* poetry of Basho (1644–1694), we have only the interpretation made by Odin (1986) concerning the transitions made in Basho's work from one sense modality to another. For instance, he quotes as 'an intensely synaesthetic experience of nature' the following:

> As the bell tone fades,
> Blossom scents take up the ringing,
> Evening shade.

Odin suggests that 'the reverberating sound of a fading bell tone merges with the fragrant perfume of flower blossom, which in turn blends with the shadowy darkness of evening shade'.

Other examples of Basho's *haiku* also imply some synaesthetic perception, e.g.

> What luck!
> The southern valley
> Make snow fragrant.

The earlier definition we provided of individuals with synaesthesia stressed that auditory stimulation *at once* gives rise to the visual synaesthesic percept. This definition arises

from the hundreds of identical descriptions we have collected from individuals from around the world who have
corresponded with us about their synaesthesia. Thus the
gradual progression from the ringing of the bell tone to the
'ringing' of blossom scents suggests that Basho is using
metaphor rather than actually experiencing synaesthesia.
This does not necessarily mean that Basho did not have
synaesthesia; simply that there is no conclusive evidence
either way.

Richard Feynman (1918–1988)

> When I see equations, I see the letters in colors – I don't
> know why. As I'm talking, I see vague pictures of Bessel
> functions from Jahke and Emde's book, with light tan j's,
> slightly violet-bluish n's and dark brown x's flying around.
> And I wonder what the hell it must look like to the students
> (p.59).

This quotation, taken from the Nobel prize-winning
physicist Feynman's book *What do you care what other
people think?*, suggests that he may well have experienced
coloured hearing synaesthesia. To the best of our knowledge Feynman was never interviewed or tested for synaesthesia, but the brief account given above is very reminiscent
of the kinds of descriptions given by bona fide synaesthetes.

Unrelated to his possible synaesthesia, but of interest is
the title chosen for his book. 'What do you care what other
people think?' turns out to have been Feynman's and his
wife, Arline Greenbaum's, *cri du coeur*. Their story is somewhat tragic as, after falling in love at first sight, they spent a
few happy years together before she died from tuberculosis.
So in love was Feynman that he married her after she was
diagnosed as fatally ill with the disease and cared for her
until her death.

David Hockney (1937-)

David Hockney, originally a British 'Pop' art painter, may well be the world's greatest living synaesthete, though to the best of my knowledge he has never been formally tested. Richard Cytowic spent some time conversing with him about the nature of his synaesthesia and the impact it has upon his work. Hockney has worked in a number of artistic media, rising to fame as an artist, subsequently with photography and later engaging in travel writing, such as his *China Diary*, published in 1981. A more recent direction has been the designing of sets for operatic productions, including Stravinsky's *The Rake's Progress* (1975) and Mozart's *The Magic Flute* at the Glyndebourne Festival in 1978. From Cytowic's account it was the designs that he developed for the 1980 program at New York's Metropolitan Opera, including works by Satie, Poulenc, and Ravel, that highlighted the fact that the inspiration he receives for his work is from synaesthesia. In an interview with CBS Cytowic gives the following account of Hockney's synaesthesia inspiration:

> Now others, David Hockney for example, the British painter, is one of my research patients, and David really didn't know that there was anything unusual about his synesthesia until he began painting opera sets, that he began painting paintings to be watched while you listen. For example, he did a series of three French operas at the Met. in New York, and the critics said, 'Well this is unlike anything he's ever done, and the colours and the shapes are so strange.' And Hockney said, 'Well I listened to the Ravel music and there's a tree in one part of it, and there's music that accompanies the tree,' and he said, 'When I listened to that music, the tree just painted itself' you see. So for him, it's an additional thing that helps to inform his art, but it's not the driving force of it.

Figure 20 Richard Feynman. (Caltech publications office)

A fascinating account and one that neatly illustrates the role that synaesthesia can have in the creative process. As far as I am aware Cytowic has never formally evaluated Hockney with tests of genuineness or brain imaging, and so we cannot be sure of the precise nature of Hockney's synaesthesia, but the suggestion is that it is a variant of hearing to vision synaesthesia. It would be intriguing to know more.

If not synaesthesia then what?

Well, conceivably synaesthesia's close-bosomed friend, metaphor. In poetry and prose metaphor is typically used more inventively. Take, for example, the following quote taken from A. S. Byatt's wonderful *Still life*, in which a dinner party guest, amidst a conversation concerning colour–letter associations, asks about the associations made for the letter 'I':

> Hodkiss said it brought to mind Henry James's simile for the dress of Sarah Pocock, 'scarlet like the scream of someone falling through a skylight'.

A rich metaphor, but maybe a connection between red and forms of danger, a well known conjunction in nature? Whatever the case, the quote serves to illustrate the point that colour can be used to convey a feeling. This technique finds equally high expression in the work of John Keats. Take as an example *The Eve of St. Agnes*, a story of two star-crossed lovers, Madeline and Porphyro. We know from Keats' selection of the name Porphyro, Greek for purple, that the poem is designed to convey passion. For Keats, this is the colour of passion, as illustrated by the thought of watching Madeline undress makes 'purple riot' in his 'pained heart'. Porphyro intends to sneak into Madeline's chambers to live this thought. His stratagem succeeds so that 20 stanzas later we read:

> Beyond a mortal man impassioned far
> At these voluptuous accents, he arose,
> Ethereal, flushed and like a throbbing star.

Hmm. Small wonder that his publishers were concerned that the text was too raunchy or, as the publisher himself wrote, 'Porphyro acts all the acts of a bona fide husband'!

Let's return to John Keats again and ask his heartfelt rhetoric: 'Do not all charms fly at the mere touch of cold philosophy?' Sadly so, synaesthetes all or synaesthetes none, one can pay one's money and take one's choice but, on the available evidence, for my money dear Vladimir is the one good candidate.

CHAPTER 6

Through a cloudy lens

Every now and then a whole branch of science bounds forward because of a new technological breakthrough. Think, for example, of the discoveries that were made possible by the invention of optical devices that could make small things bigger. Galileo's (1564–1642) telescope gave us an understanding of the night sky and Anton van Leeuwenhoek's (1632–1723) first scientific use of the microscope revealed to us flora and fauna of whose very existence we were unaware. These developments hugely increased our understanding of the world and its place in the universe.

Neuroscience has also benefited from the invention of microscopy, and in the last hundred years the ever expanding list of adjunctive techniques has allowed us to deepen our understanding of nerve cells and their interactions. However, a limitation of the use of microscopy to further our understanding of brain function has been the availability of suitable material. Traditionally we have only been able to examine dead brain tissue, obtained from either living individuals (biopsy) or dead ones (autopsy). What we really needed was a technology that allowed us to examine the human brain *in vivo*. Fortunately, techniques with their roots in late nineteenth century discoveries provided us with these much-needed techniques, as is discussed in the next section.

Here's looking through you

In 1894, Professor Wilhelm Conrad Röntgen (1845–1923) was working at the University of Wurzburg studying a scientific 'hot' topic of the day, cathode rays. These rays were generated in glass vacuum tubes into which electrodes had been embedded. When electricity was applied to these electrodes brief colourful flashes were observed in the tubes, a phenomenon we now know to have been streams of electrons. On Friday 8th November 1895, Röntgen was working on a further round of cathode ray experiments. On this occasion he appears to have found the flashes of light distracting and so placed a screen of black cardboard around the cathode ray tube apparatus. After having done this, Röntgen noticed a faint glow about a yard away from the apparatus, too far away to be accounted for by the cathode rays, which were in any case incapable of penetrating the cardboard screen. Röntgen lit a match and discovered that the glow was coming from a small phosphorescent screen on a nearby table. But the mystery remained, what could account for the glow? Röntgen, as a good scientist, repeated the experiment over and over again, seeking to determine what objects these hitherto invisible rays were capable of penetrating. Books, card, and sheets of aluminium proved ineffective barriers. Only a small lead disc seemed capable of stopping the progress of the rays. The small disc's capacity to halt the rays was interesting, but what was altogether more extraordinary was that, as Röntgen held the small disc in front of the screen, an image of the bones of his hand appeared! Röntgen worked obsessively on this amazing finding, seeking to characterize the effect as accurately as possible. Finally he revealed all to his wife, Bertha, by taking her into the lab and, with her cooperation, making the first X-ray photograph by sending the mysterious beam though her hand and then capturing the image on a photographic plate. In 1901 Röntgen was awarded the first Nobel prize for physics, recognition for his discovery of the rays he prefixed with 'X' because of their puzzling nature. X has continued to be used as the prefix for mysterious issues, as any fan of TV sci-fi can confirm.

Very dense tissue such as bone blocks lots of X-rays, whereas soft tissue, like the brain, blocks a bit less, and fluid even less than that. Consequently, X, or Röntgen, rays were capable of imaging soft tissue, but the resolution of the resulting images was too poor to be of much practical use. Nevertheless, the technique had considerable promise and clinical researchers held out the hope of one day being able to capture high quality images of the soft tissues of living individuals. The refinement of a second major invention of the twentieth century, the computer, provided the means by which the power of X-rays could be harnessed in the service of soft tissue imaging. In 1967, Sir Godfrey Hounsfield (1919–), whilst working at EMI's Central Research Labs in London, conceived a plan to image tissue. His plan involved passing hundreds of X-ray beams through a part of the body from different angles and then measuring the strength of the beam and calculating how much had been absorbed en route. These patterns of X-ray absorption could then be combined mathematically to yield a three dimensional image of the body part in cross sections, or slices. With the theory and mathematical operations ready, Hounsfield was ready to develop a prototype, but had to wait a few years until computer technology could provide a processor capable of carrying out the required operations. Finally, in 1972, EMI Ltd introduced the first commercial computerized axial tomography, or CAT scanner. Hounsfield was rewarded for his work with a Nobel Laureate in 1979, together with Alan Cormack (1924–), who, unknown to Hounsfield, had published a mathematical model for combining multiple X-ray images in 1963.

Nuclear magnetic resonance imaging

The next major step forward in imaging technology provided us with the means to obtain highly detailed structural images of the brain, but without the need to use X-rays. This technique was an application of Felix Bloch (1905–1983) and Edward Mills Purcell's (1912–1997) discovery of nuclear magnetic resonance (NMR), a discovery for which they were rewarded with Nobel Laureates in 1952. The essence of their discovery was that protons in hydrogen atom nuclei generate a signal when placed in a magnetic field. Years later, during the late 1960s, Ray Damadian (1936–) noticed that the NMR signal emitted from cancerous tissue was different from that emitted by healthy tissue. Damadian supposed that this difference could be exploited to provide a method of imaging brain tissue *in vivo* and, in 1977, Damadian and his team successfully produced a magnetic resonance imaging (MRI) scan of the whole human body. MRI scanners work by placing the person into a magnetic field thousands of times more powerful than the earth's gravitational pull. This magnetic field causes the protons in hydrogen atom nuclei to align with the field. The MRI scanner then produces a pulsed radio wave that briefly knocks the protons out of alignment. As these protons move back into alignment with the magnetic field they emit a weak electromagnetic radio signal. Signal strength is dependent upon the proton content of the tissue, which in bone is quite low, and thus bone tissue emits very little signal. In contrast, fat has a very high water content and so emits a comparatively strong signal. The MRI machine detects these differences and builds an image based on the relative strength of the signals.

From structure to function

Techniques for imaging the brain have been of immense help to scientists and clinicians who needed to be able to examine the structure of the brain *in vivo*. Access to highly detailed images of the living human brain has greatly assisted the diagnosis and understanding of brain injury caused by stroke, tumour, etc. They are useful as 'structural' images, rather like photographs of the damage. However, what researchers really wanted to do was to image the brain as it was working, to examine function rather than structure.

The key question in terms of understanding the brain is not so much the structure of different brain regions but their functions. It is taken to be axiomatic that, if the cell architecture varies between different brain regions, then the functional role played by these regions is likely to be different. Structure–function relationships tend to be the main investigational thrust of contemporary neuroscience and, to further our understanding of this relationship, we need to study the working brain.

The new technology

A number of techniques now exist to examine brain activity and in the following section a brief explanation is provided for each. A common theme in all the techniques is an assumption that brain regions burn up oxygen as they work harder. Therefore we make the assumption that, if blood flow to a region is seen to increase, this is an indication that it is involved in the activity in which the participant is currently engaged. As it is the regional variation that is of interest, the variable measured is known as regional cerebral blood flow, usually abbreviated to rCBF. At least three different rCBF measurement techniques have been used to study brain function and in the following section each technique is described using studies of synaesthetes to illustrate. MRI features again in this story, but we will begin with the earliest developments within this field and the first functional imaging technique to be used in synaesthesia, single photon emission computerized tomography, or SPECT.

The power of one – using Xenon 133 SPECT to uncover the neural substrates of synaesthesia

Michael Watson, the focus of Richard Cytowic's book *The Man Who Tasted Shapes*, was studied using one of the first functional brain imaging techniques. The procedure begins with the introduction of xenon gas that has been radioactively labelled, hence the xenon-133 nomenclature. This substance can be either injected or inhaled and, because it is inert, does not undergo any chemical transformation during its passage through the body. Xenon-133 decays quite slowly, so much so that after 5.2 days only half of the radioactivity has been emitted (i.e. a half-life of 5.2 days). To monitor changes in rCBF, highly sensitive detection devices are placed around the participant's head. These devices detect photons that are emitted from molecules of

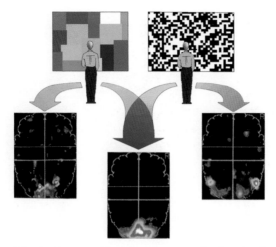

Plate 1 Zeki's visual areas. This figure represents the functional specialization known to occur in human visual processing areas. Colour processing occurs in the human V4 area and the processing of motion occurs in human V5. All retinally derived visual stimuli are processed by primary visual areas V1 and V2. Reproduced with permission of La Recherche.

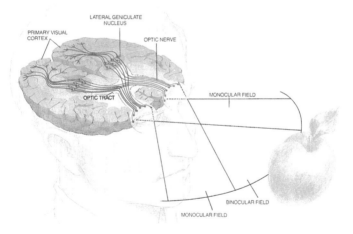

Plate 2 Visual pathway in the adult demonstrates the segregation of axons. The axons corresponding to the right eye are in red, and those corresponding to the left eye are in blue. Neighbouring retinal ganglion cells in each eye send their axons to neighbouring neurons in the lateral geniculate nucleus. Similarly, the neurons of the geniculate nucleus map their axons onto the visual cortex. The system forms a topographically orderly pattern that in part accounts for such characteristics as binocular vision.

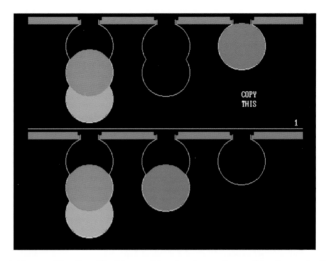

Plate 3 Tower of London. The Tower of London (sometimes referred to as the Tower of Brahma or the End of the World Puzzle) was invented by the French mathematician, Edouard Lucas, in 1883. He was inspired by a legend that tells of a Hindu temple where the pyramid puzzle might have been used for the mental discipline of young priests. Legend says that, at the beginning of time, the priests in the temple were given a stack of 64 gold disks, each one a little smaller than the one beneath it. Their assignment was to transfer the 64 disks from one of the three poles to another, with one important proviso – a large disk could never be placed on top of a smaller one. The priests worked very efficiently, day and night. When they finished their work, the myth said, the temple would crumble into dust and the world would vanish. In the example illustrated, the subject's task is: 'to make the bottom of the screen look like the top' by moving balls in the bottom half. This is an example of a one-move problem; all that is needed is to move the ball in the central pocket to the far right pocket. Reproduced with permission of CeNeS Pharmaceuticals.

xenon-133 as the compound decays. A rough map of the location from which these particles are emitted is built up, allowing judgements to be made about which brain areas are most active during the task of interest. The technique uses information about photon emission and is mapped using computerized tomography; thus this method of imaging is often referred to as single photon emission computerized tomography or SPECT for short.

SPECT xenon-133 was the technique used by Cytowic to examine the brain activity of *The Man Who Tasted Shapes* when he experienced synaesthesia. A very chatty account of the experiment can be found in the book (see Chapter 18, 'Bride of Frankenstein, Revisited') and so I shall not provide a detailed account here. However, the fundamental methodology adopted by Cytowic, the 'subtractive' method, is popular throughout neuroimaging and was also adopted by later studies of synaesthesia. In the next section the design, results, and Cytowic's interpretation of the findings are briefly described.

The subtractive method

Recent developments in the analysis of brain imaging data have increased the repertoire of techniques, but an established favourite is the subtractive method. The logic of this method is wonderfully simple. The experimenter begins by identifying the behavioural or cognitive construct of interest and selects or invents a task that will engage this construct (the 'activation condition'). In the case of synaesthesia this would mean simply exposing the participant to stimulation that elicits the experience of synaesthesia. For a colour–word synaesthete recorded speech would be adequate. The second requirement is to select a control task. A popular control task in the early days of brain imaging was to ask the participant to clear their mind and do nothing, the so-called 'resting control'. However, this is a highly unrestrained task and it soon became apparent that different participants had very different ideas about what they should do whilst 'resting'. So uncontrolled was this condition that, amongst the Institute of Psychiatry's neuro-imaging team, REST is treated as an acronym for 'random episodic spontaneous thoughts'! A more popular, and now fairly standard, control condition is to engage participants in a task that occupies them, but that does not engage the construct under investigation. To determine which brain regions act as the neural substrates for the construct of interest, one merely subtracts the rCBF seen in the control task from that observed in the activation condition.

In the SPECT investigation of Michael Watson's (MW) synaesthesia, the resting control was used and was the first condition under which his brain was imaged. Cytowic then used two activation conditions, the first of which involved administering synaesthesia-eliciting odours. The second condition was identical to the first activation condition, but this time amyl nitrate was also administered, a substance that MW had previously reported to have the property of enhancing his synaesthesia.

The results of this study are reported as being extraordinary, primarily because in the resting condition MW's rCBF varied hugely across the 16 regions of interest. However, most puzzling was the observation that his blood flow levels were uncommonly low. The comparison with the activation conditions served to deepen the mystery; blood flow in MW's left hemisphere further reduced by 18%. Unexpected decreases in blood flow in the activation condition of an imaging study are not unusual, but the magnitude of the effect seen in MW makes this an unusual finding.

Cytowic's interpretation of this observation was that synaesthesia was localized not to the cortex, but to the limbic brain, structures deep within the temporal lobes. As Cytowic himself comments:

> The final arbiter is none other than the limbic system, buried deep within the temporal lobe. It is deep enough that its metabolic activity is beyond the range of the blood flow method to measure it.

Unfortunately there is no direct evidence that synaesthesia can be localized in the limbic brain, as the technique is incapable of satisfactorily imaging deep brain structures. This deficiency is because of the relatively low energy of the photons emitted as a result of the decay of xenon-133 SPECT. Consequently, photons emitted from deep brain structures are often attenuated, making these brain regions difficult to image, even with highly sensitive equipment. A further limitation to the use of SPECT is its poor spatial resolution, i.e. the accuracy with which individual brain structures can be resolved.

Figure 22 shows the relative spatial and temporal resolution of a number of techniques and, as you can see, SPECT fares relatively poorly, especially when compared to the next technique we will consider, positron emission tomography, or PET.

It's a long shot – but it might just work...

An interesting consequence of working with psychologists and other neuroscientists is that one soon becomes aware of the different types of scientific evidence preferred by each of the two groups. As a general rule, psychologists are best

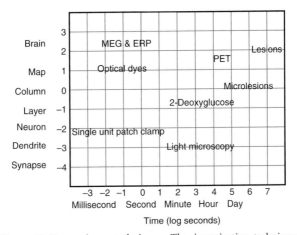

Figure 22 Neuroscience techniques. The investigative techniques used by neuroscientists. Reprinted with permission from Churchland PS and Sejnowski TJ (1988) Perspectives on cognitive neuroscience. *Science*, **242**, 741–5. American Association for the Advancement of Science.

impressed by behavioural data, the measurement of 'what people do'. Other neuroscientists seem best satisfied by physical 'objective' evidence, especially pictures of brains. We found that the behavioural data went some way towards persuading psychologists that there was something of interest here. However, our experience of presenting to neurologists was that they found such evidence much less persuasive. Therefore, the next obvious step in our research was to look for evidence that the brains of synaesthetes showed different patterns of activity (i.e. blood flow) to those of non-synaesthetes. It would have been possible to conduct SPECT studies at Charing Cross, where a SPECT facility existed. However, we were keen to resolve deep brain structures that we knew were beyond the relatively modest levels of SPECT's spatial resolution. Fortunately, just up the road, in the grounds of the

Hammersmith Hospital, was the UK's premier research facility for conducting experiments using PET – the Medical Research Council's Cyclotron Unit.

PET provides good spatial resolution as well as the capacity to resolve deep brain structures. However, PET studies are expensive to carry out, around £2000 per participant at the time we were seeking to conduct the study. Consequently, time in the scanner was very precious and researchers seeking to conduct research using it had to make an excellent case for doing so. Fortunately, Simon Baron-Cohen and I were granted the opportunity to argue our case at the locally famous 4.00 pm Friday afternoon lecture. These presentations had something of a reputation for being a robust, sometimes brusque, forum for discussing research findings. However, it was also an opportunity to persuade others that our ideas were worthy of exploration.

Amongst those present that Friday were three individuals who all decided to champion our proposal, Professor Christopher Frith, Professor Richard Frackowiak, and Professor Semir Zeki. Professor Zeki is a noted visual scientist who has made the study of the visual system the main focus of his research. His work has indicated that the various components of vision, colour, form, and motion appear to have reliably different neural substrates. Evidence already existed to suggest that selective brain lesions could deny the unfortunate recipient of the capacity to see colour (achromatopsia, 'an absence of colour vision'). Crucial to Professor Zeki's thesis was the notion that these components of vision could be selectively removed. Of particular interest to him were the reports suggesting that synaesthetes' percepts were pure colour without form. Shortly after our presentation Oliver Sacks reported the case of a New York painter who had lost his colour vision after an apparently minor road traffic accident.

What made this account of particular interest was the observation that the accident also robbed him of his synaesthesia.

Professor Frith's view on the importance of our study is particularly interesting and subsequently profoundly influenced my own view of the utility of brain imaging. A criticism of much of the published data collected using PET is that it hasn't told us anything new. For example, we have known for some time that certain brain regions are connected with specific cognitive functions. As we saw in Chapter 3, more than hundred years ago Paul Broca and Carl Wernicke implicated different regions in the production and comprehension of speech. A number of PET studies have since confirmed this, but that's all they have done. In any case, and as already discussed, the business of psychology is the understanding of behaviour and its cognitive substrates, so why get involved in brain imaging? In Professor Frith's view there is a good reason, especially in the case of phenomena such as synaesthesia.

Objective evidence of subjective mental states

The cognitive renaissance considered in Chapter two restored discussion of mental states to the psychologist's agenda. However, this liberty comes at a cost; it is one thing to posit the existence of a hypothetical construct, but then the onus falls upon you to prove its reality. Thus, while we are free to discuss and posit the existence of hallucinations, synaesthesia, and consciousness, we are then beholden to demonstrate their reality. Until recently it was accepted that, if people tell us they see colours or hear voices, then we had to take the assertion on trust. However, the burden of proof requires objective evidence, evidence that brain imaging may have the potential to provide. In the following section we will consider how such evidence was provided.

We'd like to examine your brain

One of the real pleasures of working in an international field such as neuroscience is that one is able to meet like-minded individuals from other countries. The start of our PET study of synaesthesia happened to coincide with the arrival of a husband and wife team of Italian neuro-scientists, Gabriela Bottini and Eraldo Paulesu. Paulesu was invited to join our team as lead investigator and, over the first couple of months, we hammered out the method we would use for examining synaesthesia and the technique that would be adopted for analysing the results of the study. The method settled upon relies on comparing brain activity when experiencing synaesthesia to a similar condition that does not elicit synaesthesia. We therefore chose to study individuals with synaesthesia for words but not other sounds so that we could use pure tones as our control condition. We were also aware that there might be something fundamentally different about the brains of people with synaesthesia and so we studied a group of non-synaesthetes as our control condition. We therefore had a mixed design, a within condition, and a between condition. This design is shown in the following table:

	Listening to words	Listening to tones
Synaesthetes	A	B
Controls	C	D

By convention the 'between' groups factors are listed as rows and the 'within' groups factors as columns. Labelling the conditions this way makes the description of the results easier. For example, if you subtract rCBF values for condition B from those of condition A, the resulting map would show areas active during the experience of synaesthesia. Much more interesting is the subtraction of C minus D from A minus B. Hence you can see that we are simply extending the subtractive methodology described above. There are well established techniques of analysing data but before we come to that, we shall explore how the technique is used.

Let's play PET

Essentially PET is a more sophisticated and exact method than SPECT, but one that works on the same principles. As with SPECT, participants in PET studies have a radioactive substance introduced into their bodies, usually radio-labelled water ($^{15}H_2O$). After about 30 seconds the $^{15}H_2O$ reaches the brain and begins to decay, and escaping positrons collide with electrons. These particles annihilate one another, a process that causes two photons to be emitted at 180° to one another. Around the participant's head is a ring of cameras that detect the emitted photons coincidentally, allowing for estimates to be made of the location at which the annihilation occurred (Figure 23).

Locations to which blood flow has increased will emit more photons than less well perfused regions. We know that brain cells require fuel, including oxygen, to work and so we assume that brain regions requiring increased blood flow are those working the hardest.

PET methodology has improved markedly in the last few years and it is now possible to scan participants as often as 12 times in a single session while exposing them to

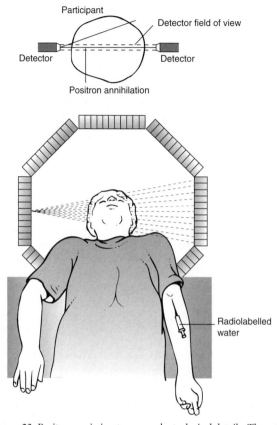

Figure 23 Positron emission tomography technical details. These two figures illustrate the procedures for administering the radiolabelled compound and the collection of data from the brain. The radiolabelled compound is injected into the bloodstream via the forearm. Approximately 30 seconds later it reaches the brain. Decaying positrons meet electrons in brain tissue and mutually annihilate in an event that releases gamma rays that are emitted at 180° from one another. These rays are detected by cameras arranged in a ring around the participant's head. Data is collected in the form of coincident detection, i.e. whether gamma rays are detected by cameras diametrically opposite to one another. The coincident detection of two rays allows an estimate of the location from which the rays were emitted to be made. In this way a map of the blood flow changes is built up.

doses of radioactivity comparable to that experienced as a consequence of living in Cornwall for a year*. Having the capacity to scan 12 times is extremely helpful, as one can choose to scan from six conditions twice to two conditions six times. Conducting two conditions six times is a robust methodology in PET as, when the data is collected, an average can be taken of the six conditions to obtain a better estimate of the true effect. This was a consideration in our design, as our study was speculative and we were keen to maximize our chances of obtaining a significant effect. This concern extended to our adoption of a further precaution, blindfolding the participants in our study to reduce the amount of visual information their brains would have to process. This is not a trivial step in a PET experiment, as the participant is asked to lie in a PET scanner, prone and with restricted head movement for a period of nearly 3 hours. During this time $^{15}H_2O$ is delivered by injection every 10 minutes. Our participants appeared to tolerate this willingly and we successfully scanned six synaesthetes and six healthy non-synaesthetes. We then excitedly set about analysing our results, which are discussed later. But what did we expect to find and why? I will first discuss the hypotheses we sought to test.

---

* When one joins the Cyclotron Unit as a visiting research fellow, as I did, the induction course contains tutorials from various experts around the unit. During the course of these induction tutorials one learns about all aspects of PET scanning, and especially the safety aspects of working with radioactive substances. During my chat with one of the physicists he provided me with various reference comparisons for the amount of radioactivity received by participants in PET studies. One of the reference comparisons was the one listed above. It seems that the granite in the West Country contains radon, a radioactive gas, which provides a small background level of constant exposure to residents.

H$_1$

As you may recall from consideration of experimental design in Chapter 4, scientific method requires that one has a hypothesis to test before conducting an experiment. Most often the established literature provides some guidance as to what one might expect, but when little or no previous work has been conducted it is hard to predict what one will find. Fortunately, a colleague from the Royal London Medical School, Dr Christian Lueck, had previously conducted a PET experiment designed to establish where the colour centre is located in the human brain. In fact it seems likely that several areas are involved in processing colour, but a critical location would appear to be the lingual and fusiform gyri, as it was these areas that tended to be strongly activated in Lueck's experimental participants. This finding is consistent with the location of lesions found in cases of achromatopsia (see Chapter 3). We therefore speculated that we might find these areas showing increased activation in the brains of synaesthetes during the word condition. We were in for some surprises, as is discussed shortly, but first a short introduction on the analysis and interpretation of PET data.

Interpreting PET data

Data derived from a PET experiment using the subtractive methodology are usually reported as brain areas that show statistically significant increases (or decreases) in rCBF. But how best to describe the location of these active regions? Neuroscientists have adopted a number of methods, but there are three that are particularly popular.

Coordinate mapping

Although individual brains are scanned, PET data can be analysed as group data; all that is required is for the data for each individual to be added together in one big subtraction. One problem with this is that different people's brains are of different shapes and sizes. To carry out a group analysis it is therefore necessary to put all participants' brain data into the same space. This normalization process is carried out with extremely memory-hungry computer programs that allow images to be stretched, shrunk, or enlarged into a standard space. This is obviously a slightly artificial process and, like all averaging techniques, often results in the loss of individual data patterns (more on this later). However, the greater power of group statistics allows researchers to test their theories more rigorously.

Once the rCBF maps for the two conditions have been plotted and subtracted from one another, one is left with a roughly brain-shaped blob of active areas. The task now is to describe where those blobs are located. The first step is to orientate ourselves within the brain. A convention in neuro-imaging is to do this by locating two anatomical structures, the anterior commissure (AC) and the posterior commissure (PC), and determining the AC–PC line (Figure 24).

An imaginary line is then drawn between these two locations and a plane extended either side of this line. The next step is to define a point along the line. This is achieved by drawing a perpendicular line at the point of the AC. Once this central plane and its centre point have been determined, any location within the brain can be defined by reference to three coordinates:

- x – This coordinate specifies how far to the left or right of the AC–PC line the brain region is located.

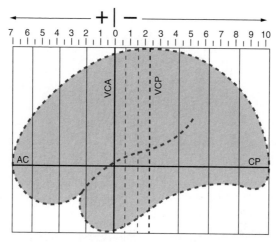

Figure 24 AC–PC line. To orientate ourselves within the brain, a baseline is drawn with reference to two well known and readily identified neural landmarks, the anterior and posterior commissures. Using this line, it is possible to label any brain region through the use of a three-coordinate system. Reproduced with permission from Talairich J & Tournoux P (1988) Co-planar stereotactic atlas of the human brain. George Thieme Verlag, Stuttgart.

- y – This coordinate determines how far forward (anterior) or toward the back of the brain (how posterior) the region is located.

- z – This coordinate specifies how high or low in the brain the region is located.

Gross anatomy

The surface of the human brain is a convoluted surface of valleys and ridges, or sulci and gyri, as anatomists call them. To be sure, there is considerable variation between individual brains, but there is a general, discernible pattern in the

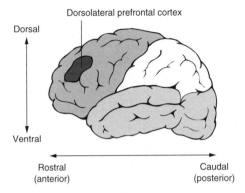

Figure 25 Dorsolateral prefrontal cortex.

location of sulci and gyri that allows similar structures to be identified in different brains. Deep brain structures are also reliably reproduced in different individuals and are delineated by different pigmentation, cellular composition, etc. Areas of the brain that can be identified and delineated using the naked eye are describable using terms from gross anatomy. These terms are often derived from descriptions based on in which lobe the structure lies, whether it is on the outside (lateral) or inside (medial) of the brain, and how high (dorsal) or low (ventral) the location is. To illustrate this better, let us consider the example shown in Figure 25.

The figure is based on a similar figure published in Owen *et al.*[†]. I have added some axes to the original figure to assist with the example. Rostral and caudal are some-

---

[†] Owen, A. M., Evans, A. C., and Petrides, M. (1996). Evidence for a two-stage model of spatial working memory processing within the lateral frontal cortex: a positron emission tomography study. *Cerebral Cortex*, 6, 31–8.

times referred to as anterior and posterior, respectively. The aim of the Owen *et al.* study was to establish the brain areas involved in working memory, the memory system in which we store items with which we need to work. The experimenters identified increased rCBF in the brain region described neuroanatomically as the dorsolateral prefrontal cortex. This region is prefrontal because it is located at the very front of the brain in the anterior portion of the frontal lobes. It is described as dorso (short for dorsal) because it is quite high up on the dorsal–ventral axis. Finally, it is lateral because it is on the outside of the brain. If the region was on the inside surface (i.e. between the hemispheres), it would be medial.

Brodmann areas

Reference to the Brodmann areas is a way of delineating functional differences between 'blobs' of rCBF change. This is a modern manifestation of the axiom that structural differences probably reflect functional differences. More on this in a bit, but let's start with an account of how the Brodmann areas came to be.

Earlier in the chapter we considered the proposition that advances in science were often facilitated by new techniques. Turn of the century microscopy was an excellent example of this. The invention of the microscope allowed us to view small objects with a hitherto unknown resolve. However, it was still difficult to tell one component of a nerve cell (neuron) from another, until light microscopists developed techniques for staining tissue samples so that these different components could be resolved by their differential susceptibility to staining. Thus it was that the turn of the century saw a number of new cell staining techniques. For example, using Nissl staining, invented by Dr Franz Nissl (1860–1919), one could selectively view Nissl granules. Alternatively, if one wanted to view neuro-

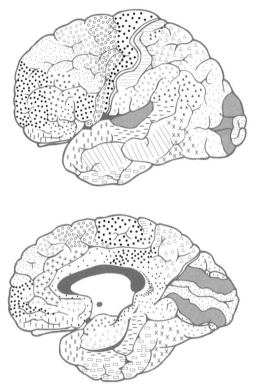

Figure 26 Brodmann areas. The diagrams show Brodmann's well known illustrations from his 1909 monograph. Brodmann divided the cortex into 47 areas, based on the differences in cell architecture. It has been observed that four regions are missing, specifically those that one would expect to be labelled as areas 13–16. It is presumed that the areas were likely to have been used to delineate the insula, a structure obscured by other structures located at area 44. However, this remains a hypothesis.

glia one could enhance their visibility using a staining method developed by Dr Camillo Golgi (1843–1956).

Neuroscience was able to make a number of advances, one discovery being that cortical areas of the human brain all contained essentially the same types of cells. However, it was also discovered that different brain regions had different cellular organization, i.e. different 'cytoarchitectures'. An obvious but painstaking task was for someone to characterize these architectures to determine how many varieties of cytoarchitecture could be found. A natural extension of this task would be to map out the cortex to show which architectures were to be found in the various cortical regions. This work fell to Dr Korbinian Brodmann (1868–1918), who published an account of his work in 1909. On the basis of his examinations he managed to divide the cortex into a total of 47 regions, though a curiosity is that, if one carefully examines Figure 26, it is apparent that areas 13 through to 16 are missing, a mystery that remains with us even today.

This amazing feat of industry, a process that delineated the human brain in different cytoarchitectonic fields, is still the basis for functional localization in the cortex today. Fortunately we now have access to a translation of the original book entitled *Vergleichende Lokalisationslehre der Grosshirnrinde in ihren Prinzipien dargestellt auf Grund des Zellenbaues*, thanks to Professor Laurence Garey, Professor of Anatomy at Imperial College Medical School.

It is, of course, sensible to ask a number of critical questions. Three obvious questions are probably:

1. Are these Brodmann areas reliably found in roughly the same location in different individuals?

2. Can these different cytoarchitectures be reliably distinguished from one another?

3. Do differences in structure genuinely reflect differences in function?

Well, the answers in brief are:

1. Sort of
2. Mostly
3. Perhaps.

Given this uncertainty, it is reasonable to ask whether identifying functional differences with specific Brodmann areas is a scientifically reasonable endeavour. As the cyto-architecture of any brain region can only be reliably established by microscopy, we clearly cannot be sure. However, it is extremely tempting (indeed, often too tempting) to speculate. An element of caution is, of course, sensible and so in our PET study, while we yielded to temptation we also attached a caveat, specifically that:

> It should be remembered that Brodmann's areas topography can not be precisely defined in life and may be insufficient to identify an activated area.

You have been warned. So much for the methods, let us move to what we actually found.

The PET study results

You might remember from the design that the critical comparison was to subtract words minus tones for control rCBF maps from the same subtraction carried out with synaesthetes. We hypothesized that the so-called human 'colour' centre would show activation as well as other areas involved in colour processing. Was this activation found? There is good and bad news, or, as they say in US government publications, good and accompanying news.

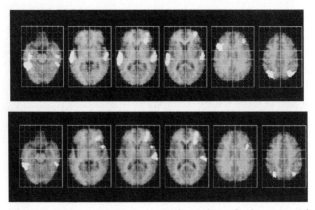

Figure 27 Positron emission tomography study results shown as axial slices through the brain. These images are 'slices' through the human brain showing as bright white patches those areas activated in synaesthetes listening to words as compared with controls. These areas include: [1] left inferior temporal cortex, [2] right prefrontal cortex, [3] the insula, [4] superior temporal cortex, and [5] the parieto-occipital junctions bilaterally. Reproduced with permission from Pavlesu E *et al.* (1995) The physiology of coloured hearing. *Brain*, **118**: 661–76. Oxford University Press. Oxford.

Anatomical location	Broadmann areas	X	Y	Z
Left posterior inferior temporal gyrus	20/37	−54	−42	−16
Left superior occipital gyrus/ superior parietal lobule junction	19/7	−16	78−	32
		−30	−62	40
Right superior occipital gyrus/superior parietal lobule junction	19/7	26	64−	40
Right middle frontal gyrus	46/10	30	50	8
Right inferior frontal gyrus	44/9	36	8	28
Right insula	−	40	8	0
Right superior temporal gyrus	22	54	−10	4

As you can see, from Figure 27 the hypothesized human colour area was not one of the areas reported. In fact, we did see increased blood flow to this region, but the effect did not survive testing with inferential statistics. The effects listed in the table were all statistically significant effects. How do we interpret these results? Being more than slightly sceptical by nature, my first reaction was frank astonishment that we had found any differences between the synaesthetes and the controls. Even more surprising to me were the marked increases in blood flow to brain regions known to be involved in colour processing, especially given that our participants were blind-folded. How do we set about interpreting these results? The usual, and obvious, approach is to refer to studies that have also activated these regions to see under what other circumstances they have been activated. This is what our research yielded about the two most intriguing activations.

Left posterior inferior temporal gyrus

This activation is particularly interesting, as no study of single word perception had ever activated this region. The non-synaesthete controls in our study did not show any increased rCBF to this region. However, previous studies have suggested that this region is involved when the brain must pay attention to colour. Other strands of research suggest that this area is crucial to the ability to integrate colour, language, and shape.

Left and right occipital–parietal junction

These activations are more perplexing, as the regions in which they occurred have not traditionally been linked to colour processing. However, there is evidence to show that lesions to these regions can cause a mild form of cortical colour impairment, a dyschromatopsia. Our best guess then is that this region might contain neurons sensitive to colour. An alternative view proposed by Dr Vincent Walsh, of the University of Oxford, is that in fact this regional activation relates to the form of the word stimuli, rather than their colour.

With respect to the other areas activated, we have very little idea of the significance of these rCBF changes. Perhaps future research will illuminate our understanding (see Chapter 9 for an exploration of these possibilities).

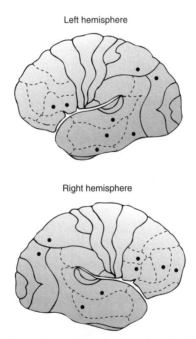

Figure 28 Positron emission tomography results as Brodmann areas. These are the same results as reported in Figure 18, but this time shown as Brodmann area activations. Reprinted from *Current Biology*, 6, Walsh V, The seeing ear, pp 389–91, 1996, with permission from Elsevier Science.

Conclusions

So, what is the bottom line here? Chiefly it is our observation that synaesthetes listening to words, whilst blindfolded, showed rCBF increases in brain areas known to be involved in either attention to colour or colour processing. However, there was no significant activation of the human colour centre. Particularly rewarding was that, as well as obtaining a robust group effect, we also saw very similar patterns of activation amongst individual members of the synaesthesia group. Often when one gets a significant between groups difference it is usually attributable to some members of the group showing a large effect. However, in this study every synaesthete showed patterns of activation consistent with the group average changes.

Based on Cytowic's single case study, we might have expected to see parts of the limbic system show increases in rCBF during the words condition. No such increase was observed. So how can we reconcile Cytowic's single participant SPECT experiment with our PET study? After all, the results of the two studies appear to be completely at odds with one another. Obviously, a group study with a more sophisticated imaging technique seems to have more credibility than a single case, but it would be inappropriate to criticize Cytowic for reporting a single case study. His situation might have been analogous to the neuropsychologists discussed in Chapter 2, trying to make the best of a bad lot, specifically a shortage of study material. One obvious possibility, previously visited in Chapters 2 and 3, is that rather than speaking of synaesthesia, we should talk of the synaesthesias. We have never encountered a case of polymodal synaesthesia and so, when considering these two studies, it is important to be aware that we are not comparing like with like. We have, as the reader might

recall, already made a case for Baron-Cohen's original participant, Elizabeth, being qualitatively different from those
examined in the group study. To me, the data simply points to
the likelihood of there being no single condition of synaesthesia, but a number of synaesthesias, all with their distinct differences, including their respective causes. This seems vague-
ly intellectually unsatisfactory, but does seem to be the most
parsimonious explanation. This would also be consistent with
our experience that polymodal synaesthetes are really rather
rare, as are synaesthetes with anything other than
colour–word synaesthesia.

We have only rarely encountered anything other than
variants of coloured hearing and so when we have encountered
individuals with other cross-modal correspondences we have
gone to great pains to study them. In the next section our experiences in testing one of these individuals, a lady with a rare
form of synaesthesia, shape–smell, and our experience of using
the most recent innovation in brain imaging, functional magnetic resonance, or fMR, are described. This section will highlight the use of a different paradigm for analysing data, related
to the single case issues explored in Chapter 3, as we will again
be seeking to interpret a single participant's performance
compared to that of a group of control participants.

The shape of smell

As previously discussed, our preferred study group has been
those with coloured hearing for words only. We have not
always had the luxury of studying any other forms of synaesthesia, largely because of a paucity of research material.
However, when the opportunity has arisen, and when time
has allowed, we have gone out of our way to study individuals
with other forms of the condition. One participant in partic-

ular (I shall refer to her by the initials AJ), who presented as a case of smell–shape synaesthesia, has been a particular focus for our studies.

Participant AJ – general information

The presentation of a synaesthete who claimed to experience shape in response to smell gave us an immediate challenge – how to design a test of genuineness for such a case? Fortunately, smell function has, for the last couple of decades, been of interest to a number of researchers, particularly those who investigate Parkinson's disease, which features olfactory loss amongst its sequelae. A consequence of this interest has been the development and sale of the smell identification test (SIT), originally by Richard Doty and others at the University of Pennsylvania.

The SIT is composed of 40 sheets, each of which has a different odour contained in microencapsulated 'scratch and sniff' patches. The action of scribbling on these patches releases the odour in a relatively uniform fashion. After the participant has deeply inhaled the emancipated odour they are asked to choose the correct answer from four possible odour descriptions, a so-called 'forced choice paradigm'. We asked AJ to identify the odour, but only as a means of testing that her olfactory function was intact. The principal appeal of using this test with AJ was to standardize the presentation of 40 smells so that for each odour we could note down her shape description. We could then present these odours for a second time and again note down the shape described so that we could compare the two for similarity. This method allowed us to construct an olfactory version of the test of genuineness. Her performance on this test is shown in the table below:

Odour	AJ	Percept description
pizza	pizza	black flex arrow from top
bubblegum	bubblegum	wide, all filling
menthol	menthol	tall shape, not quite a column, curls a bit at the top
cherry	cherry	wave shape
motor oil	motor oil	mushroom
mint	mint	flat, but not filling like bubblegum
banana	banana	round shape
cloves	cloves	spearhead shape
leather	leather	lip at bottom
coconut	coconut	spread out shape
onion	onion	collection of grids
fruit punch	fruit punch	mushroom that spirals under the cap
gingerbread	gingerbread	arrows viewed looking down on points, prickly
lilac	lilac	shaped like a drill bit
peach	peach	wide smell that tapers at the top
root beer	root beer	thin, high, rising shape
pineapple	pineapple	layers of smell together
lime	lime	flat with edges, smooth like
orange	orange	black bits, a tall smell, about 2 foot
wintergreen	wintergreen	ragged edges
watermelon	watermelon	flat dish shape, could be circle of spears
grass	grass	flat, wide smell
smoke	smoke	spearhead shape
pine	pine	upward moving
grape	grape	big and filling, like rising dough

AJ's ability to reproduce shape descriptions in response to olfactory stimulation with the odour patches of the SIT was virtually 100% accurate. Performance at this level was enough to persuade us that there was good evidence to support her claim of smell–shape synaesthesia and that it might be worth scanning her to see if we could identify the neural substrates of her synaesthesia. However, to do this we needed a control group against which to compare the pattern of AJ's brain activation. Fortunately, a solution to this challenge presented itself.

The man from Pennsylvania

More serendipitous good fortune. At about the time that we had the opportunity to test AJ, a researcher from the University of Pennsylvania, Dr David Yousem, was conducting a study designed to identify the neural substrates of odour perception and identification. We knew that his study participants were normal, healthy control participants (myself included) with no synaesthetes of any kind amongst them. We therefore planned to compare the average activation map for Yousem's study against AJ's brain mappings to determine whether there was any evidence of activation seen in her that was not characteristic of the non-synaesthete group. If any unusual activation was found in AJ, this might provide us with the neural correlate of her smell–shape synaesthesia.

Functional magnetic resonance imaging (fMRI)

You might recall from our discussion of SPECT and PET that the fundamental assumption made in functional neuroimaging is that increased rCBF implies increased brain activity in that region. Both techniques require the introduction of a radiolabelled substance into the participant's blood for the technique to work and so they are invasive procedures which are a little unpleasant to undergo. Both techniques can take quite some time to complete, and an ideal method for imaging the activity of the brain would be one that required non-invasive procedures, took relatively little time, and provided good resolution of individual brain structure. Fortunately, recent developments in MRI have provided us with a technique that accommodates these wishes.

Working brain cells require oxygen to metabolize glucose to provide energy for neurons to work successfully. Oxygen is carried by a component of the blood known as haemoglobin. A useful characteristic of oxygenated haemoglobin (oxyhaemoglobin) is that its magnetic characteristics change once the oxygen is given up and it becomes deoxy-haemoglobin. Thus the MR signal from working areas of the brain can be monitored and rCBF images built up. This blood oxygen level dependent (BOLD) imaging technique, when combined with imaging techniques such as echo planar imaging (EPI) that are capable of scanning the whole brain in just a few seconds, provides a means of quickly acquiring functional images.

Smells that have shape

Participants were first fitted with a facemask such that the nose and mouth were entirely covered, after which they were made comfortable and prepared for scanning. They were then given a 'transmission scan' to check head alignment and scanned whilst undergoing the activation and control tasks. During the 30-second activation task a sequence of three odours (clove, wintergreen, and menthol) was delivered every 10 seconds via the facemask. Participants were instructed to take a deep breath through the nose in 10-second cycles, beginning 5 seconds after the first odour delivery. This breathing rate was cued to the participant by a visual display visible from within the scanner upon which the word 'breathe' was displayed as the cue. The control condition began immediately after the activation condition, during which participants were requested to breathe at the same rate as in the activation condition. Odourless, pure air was delivered throughout the control condition. The test alternated the two conditions four times each.

The results ...

Once the data had been collected and analysed the findings were evaluated. We were all very encouraged to find that AJ was able to reproduce her first test descriptions or the 40 odours of the SIT perfectly, passing in effect a smell version of the test of genuineness. However, when we compared her blood flow maps to those of the non-synaesthete group there was no evidence of unexpected regional activation. Her brain maps contained nothing unusual.

Better news using fMRI

In addition to the study of our smell–shape synaesthete AJ, we also had the chance to further our study of coloured hearing synaesthesia using fMRI, this time with significant results. The design adopted was similar in conception to the PET study, except that this time there was a new target area to test for activation, a visual area recently identified as a brain region specialized for colour processing. The area has been christened V8, the next in what has become a long line of specialized visual (hence 'V') areas. At the time at which our PET study was performed, human visual area 6 (V6) was just being discovered. A few years later the number had risen to eight! This area had been identified using fMRI scanning of normal participants by determining which areas of the brain were activated in response to being shown coloured and monochrome visual stimuli. The activation and control conditions in the study required that the participant be shown a 'pinwheel' that induced colour or luminance changes, respectively. Blood flow maps were then compared to identify the regions showing most activation for the colour condition. The authors used a second method of activating this area by inducing colour afterimages. This ingenious approach involves scanning participants whilst they are 'seeing' an afterimage. Inducing a coloured afterimage is relatively straightforward; all one need do is have the participant stare at a saturated colour and then look at a uniform grey image. The complimentary colour is then 'seen'. For example, if a saturated red image is stared at, a green afterimage will be seen, and vice versa. The same opponency holds true for blue and yellow.

This work gave us a neat hypothesis to test with synaesthesic participants; specifically that we should expect to see activation of this area when synaesthetes listen to colour-eliciting synaesthesia (words) as compared to non-synaesthesia-inducing events, in this case pure tones. It was particularly gratifying to find precisely this outcome. Better yet, the activation was local only to the left hemisphere, which, you might recall from Chapter 3, is the linguistic hemisphere ('nous parlons avec l'hemisphere gauche'). This seems to fit; we have an area of the visual brain, apparently a substrate of colour vision, being activated in exclusively the left, linguistic hemispheres of participants with synaesthesia.

Neuroimaging work with synaesthetes continues and future studies will surely further illuminate our understanding of the neural substrates of the condition. There are always more experiments to do and we retain some ambitions regarding the neuroimaging of synaesthesia. One of these is discussed in the final chapter of this book. However, for now let's leave the neuroimaging studies to one side and evaluate what was originally Galton's theory, that synaesthesia may be a genetic condition.

CHAPTER 7

It can't be genetic, can it?

T hroughout the last few chapters we have either speculated about or cited evidence suggesting that synaesthesia might be an inherited condition, i.e. it has a genetic
component. By pure coincidence, in my email inbox this
morning was an invitation from the editor of *Nature* to visit
its web page and download a paper authored by a consor-
tium of 62 scientists from Japan, Germany, France,
Switzerland, the United States, and Britain. This paper is
something of a landmark publication as it documents the
mapping of chromosome 21, which apparently contains
less than 300 discernible genes, including several genes
linked to specific human disorders. Progress on the Human
Genome Project has been extraordinary, as have the various
technical developments that have facilitated the mapping of
the human genome, the 'blueprint' for our species. A recur-
ring theme in this book has been to highlight that much of
the contemporary literature on synaesthesia has essentially
rediscovered classical findings. The literatures differ in that
contemporary neuroscience has access to techniques
unknown to Victorian scientists. So, do we now have the
means to obtain evidence for the heritability of synaesthesia? Can we test Galton's hypothesis that 'the tendency is
very hereditary'.

Two strands of evidence suggest that pursuing the genetic route may be profitable. The first is the strongest, specifically that when individuals with confirmed evidence of synaesthesia are interviewed and asked about relatives with the condition, about 25% mention a first-degree relative. The second strand that makes one suspect a genetic basis is the huge preponderance of female synaesthetes. You may recall from Chapter 2 that we had originally supposed that this fact about synaesthesia was a modern view of the condition. However, it is clear that Krohn, writing in 1893, had also identified this fact. Richard Cytowic identified a predominance of women in his sample, a ratio of about 2.5 to 1. In our own work we have found that comfortably more than 95% of the synaesthetes we have tested have been female. This percentage also holds for the total number of individuals we had heard from, but not necessarily tested, in 1993. In all, we have been contacted by 565 individuals with synaesthesia, of which more than 95% are female. Every individual in this sample has been contacted by us and sent a questionnaire that included the question about first-degree relatives. A total of 23.4% of respondents listed a female relative. Not one single respondent listed a male relative.

So can we assume that these figures are true? The first obvious problem with such an assumption is the discrepancy between the data from Cytowic and from our own study. Cytowic reports a female:male ratio of 2.5:1, whereas our studies suggest a ratio approaching 20:1. One clear difference is that Cytowic's sample is composed of various different forms of synaesthesia, whereas the vast majority (in fact, all but a few odd cases) of our sample report having coloured hearing. There are, however, other problems with assuming that our estimates are correct, largely to do with the way in which we have selected our sample.

Ascertainment and bias

Whenever we seek to identify a population of individuals with certain characteristics it is important to be sure that the sample we select for study is representative. Think back to the example of calculating the average height of males in Chapter 3. The only way to be accurate is to measure the height of every male in the world, an impossible task. Statistics relies on measuring a subset ('sample' in statistical parlance) from the population of interest and then calculating the characteristic of interest. That finding is then extrapolated to the entire population. Clearly the estimate of the population characteristics will only be accurate if the sample is genuinely representative. As an example of where we might go awry, a pygmy statistician seeking the average height of males might be significantly inaccurate if he or she selected only from his or her tribe.

To be certain about our characterization of synaesthetes it is important to be sure that we have a truly representative sample to study. As most of our referred cases have come to us as a result of media coverage, it is distinctly likely that our sample is at least a little biased. Assuming too much about the representativeness of a sample can easily lead to false assertions being made. A good example of this was an article that appeared in the *The Independent* on 30th June, 1992. This article, entitled 'June is Blue and Pigs are Green' was an account of some of the work that had been conducted into synaesthesia. During the author's interview, Baron-Cohen mentioned that: 'We have found that most synaesthetes are bright and artistic'. This was indeed the case, but one must remember that the majority of the participants we had been contacted by were *Science on 4* listeners and therefore probably not a representative sample. Unsurprisingly, we heard from many more bright and artistic synaesthetes after the article appeared. While on this issue it is worth considering some of the other claims made about synaesthetes. For example, Richard Cytowic has found apparently high levels of poor mental arithmetic skills, a higher than expected proportion of left-handers, and the suggestion that the spatial skills of people with synaesthesia tend to be poorer than one would expect. He also notes a high frequency of homosexuality amongst his sample. Now, it is of course possible that these characteristics are true. However, it is equally possible that these observations are due to biased sampling.

Ascertaining a representative sample

To be sure about the characteristics of any population, it is important to obtain a truly representative sample. Ideally, one should target a general population and then determine what proportion has the condition of interest; in our case, synaesthesia. However, given the prevailing estimates of how common synaesthesia appears to be, the prospect of such an exercise was somewhat daunting. Richard Cytowic, for example, had in 1989 estimated that synaesthesia was found in about 1 in 250 000 individuals, thus one would need to interview one million people to obtain just four cases. Cytowic revised this estimate down to 1 in 100 000, and others estimated that it might be as common as 1 in 25 000.

Baron-Cohen determined that, in spite of this, we should seek to determine more scientifically how commonly synaesthesia is found in the population. The scientific term for the total number of cases in a population at a given time is the 'prevalence'. This is in contrast with the 'incidence'; i.e. the number of new cases in a population over a time period. To establish the minimum prevalence, two of Baron-Cohen's students, Lucie Burt and Fiona Smith-Laittan, placed the following advertisement in the *Cambridge Evening News* (*CEN*) and in the Cambridge University Student magazine *Varsity*:

> Research into synaesthesia:
> Some people experience a mixing of the senses. This is known as synaesthesia. For example, whenever they hear sounds, they automatically see colours. For other people, a different sense (touch, taste or smell) might trigger a visual or auditory experience. We are trying to find out how common this is, and would like to hear from people who think they have synaesthesia.

The advertisement was placed in both publications so that a minimum prevalence could be ascertained from Cambridge's 'town' population via the *CEN* and from the 'gown' population via *Varsity*. As a result of placing the advertisement 28 readers of the *CEN* contacted us claiming to have synaesthesia. All 28 were examined and 22 cases were confirmed, 18 of colour–word synaesthesia, and four with coloured music. The readership of the *CEN* is estimated to be about 44 000 so, on this basis, we estimated the prevalence to be about 1 in 2000. The sex ratio in this group was 6.3:1 in favour of females. Seven (33%) of the group reported having synaesthesic family members.

Varsity has a smaller readership, about 11 000, and our advert prompted only four individuals to contact us claiming to have synaesthesia. Again, all volunteers were contacted and tested to confirm synaesthesia. This level of response suggested a prevalence of 1 in 2500, comfortingly similar to the *CEN* result. Again, the majority of individuals were female (3:1 ratio) and one of the four reported a synaesthesic family member.

These findings suggest that synaesthesia is substantially more common than was previously suspected, with a probable minimum prevalence of 1 in 2000. These findings were also helpful in that they confirmed that the condition is markedly more common in females and that about 25% of cases have an affected first degree relative. Also confirmed was our suspicion that coloured hearing seems overwhelmingly to be the most common form of the condition. This observation

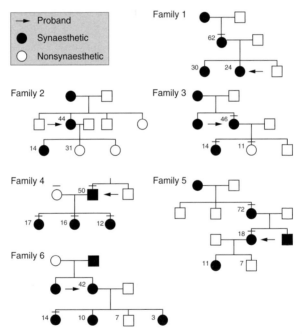

Figure 29 Synaesthesic family pedigrees from Baron-Cohen *et al.* Squares represent males, circles females. Horizontal lines indicate the individual was actually tested, rather than the information being derived solely from report. Numbers indicate the individual's age. Reprinted with permission of Pion Ltd, London from Baron-Cohen S *et al.* (1996) Synaesthesia: prevalence and familiarity. *Perception,* **25:** 1073–9.

has also been confirmed by a study of 270 cases collected by Dr Sean Day, who has found that the vast majority of cases (greater than 90%) are forms of coloured hearing.

The blood is the life

The studies detailed above suggest that the population prevalence runs at about 0.05%. We compared this to the prevalence of synaesthesia in families where the condition is shared by first-degree relatives. The familial prevalence rate in these families was found to be 48.6%. This strongly indicates the familiality of the condition. Pedigrees for these families are shown in Figure 29, together with a key to indicate what the various formal symbols used by geneticists mean.

Access to these pedigrees allows us to calculate the chances of synaesthesia occurring in the first-degree relatives of a synaesthetes' family. As you can see from the pedigree diagram, eight of the eleven daughters shown have the condition. These data show that the daughter of an affected individual has approximately a 72% probability of inheriting the condition. The pedigree also shows that just one of the four sons has been confirmed as a synaesthete, suggesting a 25% chance of a son having the condition. This is only slightly better than the probability of a brother having the condition. This stands at about 17%, based on just one case occurring in a total of six individuals. Returning to first-degree female relatives, it seems that sisters of affected individuals have a 60% chance of having synaesthesia as, in our affected families, three of the five sisters had their synaesthesia confirmed. Having mapped out in our family pedigrees we now had an organized dataset to show expert geneticists to determine whether the patterns seen in the data implied a particular mode of inheritance. So what did these experts decide? Well, several models have been proposed and these will be described shortly. However, before this, a little information about the background and reference terms of these models.

Genetics – in the beginning

A feature of academic life in the neurosciences at Charing Cross is the monthly divisional meeting, at which an internal and an external speaker present aspects of their work. Neuroscience is a very diverse research focus and attracts scientists working at all levels of the hierarchy of science. A characteristic of the presentations is that the nearer the top of the hierarchy the simpler it is to present to such a diverse audience. After all, as a psychologist one is likely to be presenting data on a behaviour shared by everyone present. Physiologists, clinicians, biologists, those working in neuroimaging, and even the physicists working on vision had a reasonably easy job presenting. Not so the geneticists. Genetic research tends to make use of a scientific vocabulary and experimental techniques peculiar to the discipline. Consequently, presentations to the hoi polloi of neuroscience presented a challenge to our brothers and sisters in the genetics teams.

I approach this section of the book with the same trepidation, partially because my understanding of the rudiments of genetics is far from complete, but also because I remember how hard it was for me to grasp the little I know! Nevertheless, the genetic models described later in the chapter will live a little more if we spend some time now explaining some of the assumptions and vocabulary of work in genetics.

The language of genetics

Many will have heard about the mapping of the human genome, but seldom in all the coverage do commentators explain quite what it is. Let us start with a definition. The human genome is the precise set of instructions needed to make a person. It is composed of inherited information stored as DNA in all human cells. DNA is organized into 46 chromosomes, 22 homologous chromosomes and a pair of autosomes, either X and Y if you are male, or X and X if you are female.

This line of research began more than a hundred years ago, when an Austrian monk by the name of Gregor Mendel (1822–1884) began experimenting with pea plants that he had classified according to the various characteristics they exhibited. Mendel had noted and organized the plants according to their flower colour, the size of the plant, and even the texture of the seedpod. Having characterized these plants he then set about crossbreeding them to see what would result. In a series of experiments Mendel established what we now know to be the principles of inheritance; in fact it is called Mendelian inheritance in celebration of Mendel's contribution. One of Mendel's discoveries, and one that is crucial for our understanding of the possible modes of inheritance of synaesthesia, was the notion of dominant and recessive genes. Mendel found that, when he crossed tall plants with the pollen of other tall plants the result was tall offspring. However, he also identified that pollinating a tall pant with pollen from a small plant also tended to yield tall offspring. Mendel decided that tallness must be a dominant trait, whereas smallness appeared to be recessive. Further experimentation revealed that smooth peas are dominant to wrinkled peas, and that red flowers are dominant to white ones.

The next step in Mendel's experiment involved fertilizing the pea plants with their own pollen. Now the recessive traits reappeared, not in equal frequency to the dominant traits, but in a 3:1 ratio of dominant to recessive. Mendel explained these results by hypothesizing the existence of 'factors', or what we would call genes. He also deduced that the observed pattern of inheritance could be explained by the presence of two genes. Under these circumstances, crossing a red-flowering (dominant trait) pea plant with a white (recessive) would tend to yield three red-flowering offspring to every white. Why should we expect this ratio? We can understand this with reference to probability, as, with two genes, there are four possible combinations.

Crossed combination	Description of traits	Resulting offspring
Red + Red	Dominant + Dominant	Red
Red + White	Dominant + Recessive	Red
White + Red	Recessive + Dominant	Red
White + White	Recessive + Recessive	White

As this table shows, the mere presence of the red flower gene is sufficient to ensure that the offspring have red flowers. Only when both genes are coding for white flowers will the offspring also have white flowers. When the two inherited genes code for the same colour we describe the organism as homozygous. When the genes are mixed we use the term heterozygous. This is a good point at which to introduce another common term in genetics, the notion of an allele. A textbook description of an allele is 'one of a number of different forms of gene'. So, in the heterozygous cases of red- and white-flowered peas, two different alleles for the flower colour gene have been inherited, one from each parent. A further definition would be to describe alleles as alternative forms of a genetic locus. In the heterozygous cases shown in the above table, the red flower

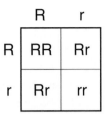

Figure 30 Punnett square. Punnett squares are named after their inventor, Reginald Crundall Punnett (1875–1967), one time Professor of Genetics at Cambridge University, and the author of the first textbook on the work and theories of Gregor Mendel.

allele is dominant over the white flower variant. The table shown above is a neat enough explanation, but geneticists would tend to plot Punnett squares, as in the above example (Figure 30).

What is most remarkable about Mendel's work is that he provided the fundamental principles of inheritance with absolutely no knowledge of the mechanisms by which these traits were inherited. We now know, thanks to the work of Walter Sutton (1877–1916), that the factors that determine our characteristics are stored in the nucleus of every cell in an individual's body as a set of chromosomes. However, Sutton's view remained theoretical until Thomas Henry Morgan and his group provided evidence that genes for many character traits are arranged in a linear fashion on each chromosome. Morgan also determined that some traits are linked to sex chromosomes. A key event was his discovery of a white-eyed male fruit fly that provided him with the opportunity to crossbreed his white-eyed male with a red-eyed female. Morgan found that the resulting offspring were all red-eyed. However, self-crossing the white-eyed male yielded 3470 red-eyed flies and 782 white-eyed, all of whom were males, for the first time demonstrating a sex-linked trait. Morgan became progressively more and more interested in species variation and, in 1911, he established the 'Fly room' to investigate how a species changed over time. For the next 17 years, working in an apparently very unpleasant, smelly room measuring a mere 16 × 23 ft, Morgan and his students carried out ground-breaking genetic research using *Drosophila melanogaster*, the fruit fly. Working in such cramped and unpleasant conditions stimulated Morgan's intellect and he was awarded with the Nobel Prize for medicine in 1933.

The fly

Both Jeff Goldblum and Vincent Price have had the misfortune to have their genetic code mixed up with that of a fly, with tragic, and in Goldblum's case, quite revolting, consequences. Why has the apparently humble fly inspired geneticists and Hollywood directors alike? In the case of the latter it is presumably because flies have fairly revolting dining habits and so *auteurs* wishing to shock can use this material very profitably. Geneticists use the fruit fly so extensively in part because of precedent; someone years ago decided to study these small flies and so we now know a considerable amount of detail about the genetic make-up of these creatures. Mutant flies with defects in any of several thousand genes are available. Also, the US genomics company Celera has recently made the entire fruit fly genome available through their web site (see http://www.celera.com). A second possible appeal of studying good old melanogaster is simply that these animals are cheap and easy to keep in large numbers. Also, their life cycle is a mere 2 weeks, so any expression of new traits has only a short time to emerge.

Drosophila has four pairs of chromosomes; three autosomes and the X and Y sex chromosomes. The fruit fly genome extends to about 165 million base pairs and is estimated to contain about 12 000 genes. This stands in marked contrast to the human genome that has 3300 million bases and may have as many as 70 000 genes (yeast has about 5800 genes in 13.5 million bases).

The extraordinary double helix

Work in the 1960s revealed that chromosomes are in fact mostly just one long strand of a highly specialist molecule, deoxyribonucleic acid or DNA, a simple structure that gives rise to extraordinary complexity. So simple is the structure of DNA that, for most of the first half of the last century, many scientists believed that the proteins found in the nucleus were the determining genetic influence. DNA was thought to be merely the supporting scaffold. However, work by Oswald Avery (1877–1955) unequivocally showed that genetic information is carried in DNA rather than by the proteins of the cell. At the time of his discovery Avery was in fact investigating the process of 'transformation' in bacteria, a phenomenon, unexplained at the time, where tiny capsules form in a bacterium that previously had none after the bacterium was exposed to a substance from bacteria containing similar capsules. Avery noticed that the change in the bacteria was heritable, and determined that the substance that came into contact with the bacteria contained the genes causing the development of capsules. He later determined this substance to be DNA.

What remained undetermined was how the molecule coded this complexity, made as it was of deoxyribose sugar, a phosphate group, and four nitrogen bases, adenine, thymine, guanine, and cytosine. In possibly one of the most famous discoveries in science, James Watson and Francis Crick, working at the Cavendish laboratory in Cambridge, finally showed how such complexity could come from such simplicity.

Figure 31 shows the double helical structure of DNA, as discovered by Crick and Watson in 1953. The phosphates and sugars link in long strands to form a polymer. The rungs of this twisted ladder structure are provided by the linking of nitrogen base pairs. A crucial characteristic of DNA is that the nitrogen bases always link in specific pairs; adenine always links with thymine and guanine with cytosine.

The genetic factors, or genes, that Mendel posited we now know to be coded for by sequences of these adenine–thymine and guanine–cytosine base pairs. These sequences determine the production of proteins within cells, proteins that are the fundamental building blocks of what makes us the individuals we are. Our species is capable of coding more than 100 000 different kinds of proteins, each one of which is coded for by genes contained within our DNA. Mendel described a gene as a discrete unit of heredity that influences a visible trait. This is an explanation couched at a hypothetical level that can be updated at a molecular level as discrete directions for making a single protein. No mean task; the 100 000 proteins mentioned above are all coded for by different gene sequences.

Modern science has been able to locate and characterize Mendel's hypothesized constructs as the 'genetic elements', or, as we now know them, genes. We also now know that a gene is a sequence of base pairs on a strand of DNA that codes for a protein. These protein molecules are made up of building blocks known as amino acids and we also now know that three base pairs (a codon) determine one amino acid. So, for

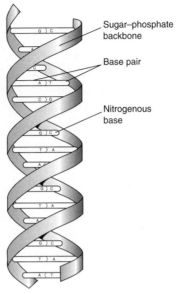

Sugar–phosphate backbone

Base pair

Nitrogenous base

Figure 31 Structure of the DNA molecule. This diagram schematic-ally represents the helical structure of DNA. The support for the molecule is provided by the sugar–phosphate backbone that holds the 'rungs' of the structure. These rungs are made of the four bases, which pair so that adenine and thymine always link with one another, as do guanine and cytosine. Individual proteins are coded for by thousands of base pair sequences.

example, the amino acid methionine is coded for with the base sequence adenine–thymine–guanine (ATG). As the average protein is comprised of 1000 amino acids, it follows that the average gene will be made up of 3000 base pairs. The maths of 100 000 genes multiplied by 3000 base pairs per gene suggests that the entire human genome should be about 300 000 000 base pairs. However, we estimate that the genome in fact contains as many as 3 billion base pairs. Why so many base pairs and so few genes?

Introns and exons

Analysis of DNA sequences has shown that within genes there are protein coding sequences (exons) interspersed with sequences that have no coding function (introns). However, introns and exons together still only account for 10% of the entire genome, so what are all those other base pairs there for? Well, we are not quite sure, but the assumption is that they are control genes, perhaps responsible for turning on and off the coding sequences. Doubtless further study of the human genome will yield greater understanding of the role of this 90% of our DNA.

This brief tutorial ends with a brief consideration of the modes of inheritance that are explored in more detail in the next section, in which the various genetic models proposed to explain synaesthesia are explored.

The genetic models of inheritance

There are three possible modes of inheritance for synaesthesia, though others may exist.

Autosomal dominant

Autosomes are those which are not sex chromosomes. In this model alleles present in one parent (of either sex) will be transmitted to 50% of sons and daughters; all who receive one copy of this allele will be affected.

Autosomal recessive

An autosomal recessive trait means that the alleles will produce, on average, 25% affected offspring of both sexes if both parents are unaffected heterozygotes. If one parent is affected and the second parent is a carrier, then 50% of their offspring will be affected, while the other 50% will be carriers.

Sex-linked dominant/recessive

It is sex chromosomes that determine our gender, with two X chromosomes yielding a female and an X and a Y giving a male. Dominant and recessive have the same implications here as in the autosomal models of inheritance discussed above.

Two geneticists write...

A helpful review of the possible models of inheritance was carried out by two Charing Cross based geneticists, Mark Bailey and Keith Johnson. They considered the various models by predicting what each of them would imply for the inheritance of synaesthesia and then testing their predictions against what is known about the condition. In the case of autosomal recessive traits one would expect to see no sex difference emerge with respect to the number of offspring with the disorder. A similar difficulty exists with respect to the model of inheritance likely to be because of autosomal dominant transmission. This is the model that Richard Cytowic favoured as the most likely model; presumably this fitted with his experience of the apparent inheritance of the condition. Amongst his pedigrees Cytowic found that synaesthesia appeared to be passed down either the maternal or paternal line to offspring of either sex and with no skipped generations. However, this model sits ill with the repeated observation (including Cytowic's own cases) that the condition is far more prevalent amongst women. Bailey and Johnson were unwilling to rule out this model as it is possible that the condition may have reduced expression in males.

The predominance of female synaesthetes in papers from Krohn to Baron-Cohen *et al.* demands that potential models of inheritance explain the female to male ratio. Given this, the view of both Bailey and Johnson, and Baron-Cohen *et al.* is that the best fit for the data is a model that is linked to the X chromosome and inherited as a dominant trait. If synaesthesia is inherited as an X-linked dominant condition, this would mean that there would be a sex bias as high as 3:1 (female:male). This is because, in X-linked conditions, heterozygous females will transmit the trait to half their offspring of both sexes. Males would transmit to all female offspring and no male offspring. Ostensibly, then, a possible solution. However, the female:male ratio is usually reported to be much higher than 3:1; in fact, it is usually closer to 6:1. To match this ratio of transmission it is necessary to incorporate one more effect into the model, the possibility that the gene might be lethal in some male offspring.

Sex-linked dominant, with lethality in males

To produce a model that accommodates a female:male ratio of over 3:1 we need to provide for the possibility that the gene, if it exists, causes 50% of the male fetuses to die *in utero*. But how plausible is this notion; after all, it seems to be a dramatic caveat to add to our simple X-linked dominant model of inheritance. Interestingly, it appears to fit the available data. Take a glance back to Figure 19, the pedigrees of our synaesthesic families, and count up the number of offspring confirmed as having synaesthesia. To save you the bother, there are 18 females and 9 males. This is precisely what one would expect if hemizygous males are unlikely to survive.

There are other aspects of the available data that are consistent with this model. For example, the proportion of affected offspring from maternal transmissions is a little over 50%, just as the model predicts under this mode of inheritance. Also, because the transmission is linked to the X chromosome, one would expect to see high levels of transmission from synaesthesic fathers to affected daughters. Again, the data supports this, with five out of five cases showing this transmission. The model also requires that there must be no instances of male-to-male transmission, as male offspring receive their X chromosome from their mother, which, again our data supports. This condition of the proposed synaesthesia model of inheritance is interesting to contemplate in the context of one of our 'usual suspects' from Chapter 5. You might recall that of all the famous synaesthetes, the one individual who sounded like the genuine article was the novelist Vladimir Nabokov? Dear Vladimir was blessed with a synaesthesic father, which is neither a sufficient nor necessary condition for Vladimir to inherit the condition. However, we also know that Nabokov's mother was a synaesthete, circumstances that fit with our favoured model. Perhaps the most important observation is simply the repeated observation that the ratio of female to male synaesthetes tends to be markedly in excess of the 3:1 that simple X-linked dominant transmission would yield.

None of the predictions that follow from the adoption of this model are disconfirmed by the available data, though it would, as ever, be prudent to conduct considerable further research, with a larger sample, to test this model.

So, is it genetic?

It seems remarkable, but it would appear to be distinctly likely that synaesthesia is inherited, just as Galton suggested more than a hundred years ago. However, perhaps it would be more accurate to suggest that the circumstances under which synaesthesia can occur are inherited. How do we go about finding evidence in support of our proposed genetic model of synaesthesia? The means to do so may already be at hand. As Bailey and Johnson remind us, one prediction arising from the X-linked dominant with lethality in males model is that there should be an increase in the rate of miscarriage amongst women with synaesthesia. We currently have no data on this, but such a study could potentially provide some supporting evidence for the preferred inheritance model.

The methods by which one hunts for a gene are complex indeed, and far beyond the remit of a humble little book like this. Extraordinary developments in our capacity to break the code of the human genome occur almost daily. It seems that we shall shortly complete the sequencing of the base pairs that make up the human genome, an important first step in understanding the rules for making humans. The sophistication of the techniques and technology available to scientists in both the public and private sectors mean that huge amounts of dull and hugely labour intensive research activity can be automated. An indication of the efficiency of this technology was recently demonstrated when a number of labs were given the opportunity to use software programs designed to identify genes on part of the fruit fly genome. They managed to identify between 86 and 97% of the protein coding sequences in this chunk of genetic information. Just as computers facilitated the development of brain imaging, they have now been used to good effect in our determination and understanding of the contents of the human genome. Work of this kind has recently been christened with a new term, *in silico*, to denote that this form of biological modelling occurs in 'organisms' made from silicon, namely computers. This is another in a long line of Latin terms used to describe where a biological experiment or analysis is conducted. Previously science had adopted *in utero* to describe events happening in the womb, *in vivo* to describe events occurring in the body, and *in vitro* to describe those occurring outside the body.

The combination of knowledge and technology is of course helpful, but, to determine (a) the likelihood that synaesthesia is indeed inherited, and (b) explain the mechanisms by which this occurs, requires the addition of two further ingredients; raw material, in this case the DNA from individuals with synaesthesia, and some ingenuity. As part of the procedure for the prevalence and familiality study described earlier in this chapter, we also obtained blood from those synaesthetes willing to donate. This collection of blood now resides in Oxford with a team of geneticists under the leadership of Dr Tony Monaco of the Wellcome Centre for Molecular Genetics in Oxford, UK, waiting for time to present us with the opportunity to hunt for the synaesthesia gene, which begs another question – is it a gene or many genes?

Monogenic or polygenic

One of the key statistics that work on the human genome has revealed is that more than 99% of your genetic information is identical to that of anyone elses. A further remarkable statistic is the finding that 97% of the entire genome does not appear to code for proteins. This portion has attracted the highly technical term 'junk DNA' to denote its apparent unimportance. Clearly the differences between individuals are likely to be found on very specific portions of the genome. One key question is whether some of these interpersonal differences are because of variations found in one (monogenic) or many genes (polygenic). Could a single gene really influence our experience so radically as to give one group of our species the ability to perceive colour when listening to sounds? It seems a distinct possibility. We already know that disorders such as Duchenne muscular dystrophy, sickle cell anaemia, and cystic fibrosis are all due to single gene differences. We also know that colour blindness, an event that dramatically effects the way in which we can perceive the world, is due to a single gene. It might be this simple, synaesthesia could be due to a single gene difference. If this turned out to be the case, then by identifying the gene we might be able to determine the mechanism by which synaesthesia causes sense information to leak from one modality to another. If, for example, we found that the gene was expressed as a controlling factor in the process of apoptosis, then this might provide strong, direct evidence in support of our theory for a preserved neonatal connection between auditory and visual areas of the brain.

Clearly, single gene differences are much easier to find than those which are due to a number of different genes, but many conditions, diseases, and traits are likely to be due to the influence of a number of genes interacting with one another. Unravelling the impact of the multiple genetic influences upon a behaviour like synaesthesia is likely to be quite a challenge.

CHAPTER 8

Pathology and theory

A t the end of Chapter 1, in which I outlined the theory of synaesthesia proposed in *Synaesthesia: Classic and Contemporary Readings*, I promised to describe and evaluate other theories that have been posited by various individuals during the last hundred years. In previous chapters, especially Chapters 2 and 3, it was suggested that there is evidence to suppose that certain brain injuries and diseases are capable of causing synaesthesic states. A number of these reports contain theories on the genesis of acquired synaesthesias, and the overlap between pathology and theory suggests that they be dealt with in the same chapter. They are discussed here, beginning with cases of acquired synaesthesia, a term used to distinguish the supposedly inherited form from the pathological forms that typically emerge some time after birth. As we will see, there are some marked differences between the acquired and inherited cases, differences that are summarized at the end of the following section. Let us begin with examples of synaesthesia apparently caused by brain injury or disease, beginning with damage to the eye, including the optic nerve.

Optic nerve and eye damage

A number of studies have reported instances of 'synaesthesia' as a consequence of visual loss involving anterior visual pathways. A good example of such a report is that made by Lessell and Cohen (1979), who describe three patients with unilateral eye, or optic nerve, disease. An important caveat to attach here is that these patients did not see synaesthesiae, but instead perceived patches of light when they heard noises. Seeing patches of light, or phosphenes as they are known to scientists, is quite a common phenomenon. Rubbing your eyes, spending a long time in the dark, or receiving a blow to the head can all bring on the experience of 'seeing stars'. In the case of rubbing your eyes it is thought that this activity exerts pressure on the optic nerve that causes impulses to be sent to the visual cortex. Phosphenes can also commonly accompany migraine attacks*. However, the visual experiences seemed much less complex than the percepts reported by synaesthetes.

A slightly more pseudosynaesthetic visual event was reported by Bender, Rudolph, and Stacey in 1982. Their patient was suffering from optic neuritis, a disorder due to inflammation of the optic nerve, often a warning sign that the patient is at risk of multiple sclerosis. This particular individual reported seeing a blue light whenever he heard a loud noise or experienced a sudden pain. Again, this visual

---

* The well published neurologist Oliver Sacks has suggested that the visual events caused by migraine attacks might be a cause of the visual experiences reported by religious visionaries. He cites the case of Hildegard of Bingen (1098–1179) who recorded 'I saw a great star most splendid and beautiful, and with it an exceeding multitude of falling stars which with the star followed southwards. ... And suddenly they were all annihilated, being turned into black coals ... and cast into the abyss so that I could see them no more.' Sacks suggests that this sounds very like the visual events that can accompany migraine.

event is a less complex percept than the synaesthesiae reported by individuals with coloured hearing. A rather more complex form of visual event was reported in a study conducted by Rizzo and Eslinger in 1989. Their study was of a 17-year-old patient who had suffered perinatal visual deprivation as a consequence of retrolental fibroplasia. This visual disorder was first reported in the 1940s and was presumed to be due to the administration of excess oxygen to premature babies. More recently, some doubt has been expressed about this putative cause as the condition has also been seen in full term babies who did not receive oxygen. Whatever the cause, the condition appears to give rise to the development of fibrous retinal tissue behind the lens, leading to a loss of vision and hence the term retrolental fibroplasia. This individual was remarkable in that he showed strong associations between musical notes and coloured shapes. Just as with the cases of coloured hearing reported earlier, specific musical notes consistently elicited the same colours, suggesting to the authors that this qualified as a case of synaesthesia.

The authors used a variety of psychophysical and neurophysiological tests, including auditorily evoked potentials (AEPs), but failed to find any remarkable or unusual results. Rizzo and Eslinger concluded that their patient's synaesthesiae were due to 'strong cross modal associative ability' rather than to unusual neural transmission. I consider their results to be inconclusive and that they could not really choose between these two possibilities. We have recently discovered that the brain is capable of remarkable reorganization when brain injury occurs early in life (recent work which shows that, in congenitally blind individuals, tactile stimulation gives rise to activation in visual areas is discussed in Chapter 9). Given this it seems distinctly likely that Rizzo and Eslinger's patient could have developed correspondences rather than associations.

An explanation for how music may have given rise to visual events has been proposed by Jacobs *et al.* in their report on nine patients with visual loss due to lesions of the optic nerve or chiasm. These patients all experienced photisms induced by sound, though in most cases the photisms appear to have been quite complex, sometimes described as 'a flame, a petal of oscillating lines, a kaleidoscope, or an amoeba'. One of the procedures adopted by the investigators was perimetry, a technique that plots the limits of the patient's visual field to highlight areas of deficiency. A remarkable finding from this procedure was that the photisms always occurred in the defective portion of the visual field. This is clearly at odds with the accounts given by our idiopathic synaesthetes, who are clear that their synaesthesiae do not occur in the visual fields. Further differences in the accounts given by patients in Jacob's study include the fact that their sound-induced photisms occur in circumstances that provoke a startle reaction to sound. The authors propose what Baron-Cohen and I have previously called 'sensory leakage theory' to explain these events, discussed in a little more detail later in this chapter. An important caveat to attach to the Jacobs *et al.* study is that close examination of the patients reported reveals that four of these patients (cases 1, 2, 4, and 7) also experienced photisms in the *absence* of auditory stimulation, casting doubt on whether these instances should be described as cases of auditory visual synaesthesia at all. It is also worth observing that seven patients always experienced their photisms when they were 'relaxed, drowsy or dozing' (p.214), circumstances in which hypnagogic hallucinations are well known to occur.

Synaesthesia as a consequence of brain tumour

Vike, Jabbari, and Maitland (1984) report seeing a man who, when stimulated with clicks of 65 decibels, saw kaleidoscopic and spiralling lights in his left eye. On removal of a large cystic mass extending from his left medial temporal region to the midbrain, his synaesthesia stopped. This is just one example drawn from the small but interesting literature that describes synaesthesia as being acquired as the result of disease or brain injury. A variety of neuropathological conditions have apparently given rise to acquired synaesthesias. In one of the earliest accounts, Carnaz (1851) speculated that synaesthesia of all forms was 'pathological and due to some optical lesion' (cited in Krohn [1893], p.33), and could therefore be seen as being due to 'hyperaesthesia of the sense of colour'. These forms of synaesthesia appear to have much less complex correspondences, but are nevertheless interesting contrasts with the inherited form. In the next few pages some of these cases are described.

Synaesthesia in psychosis

Schizophrenia plays havoc with the individual's ability to function successfully. Contrary to popular belief, schizophrenia does not mean the patient is suffering from a split personality. If there is a personality effect then it can be far better characterized as a disintegration of personality. Just as with so many other brain disorders, we do not know what causes the psychotic behaviour characteristic of the disease. Unsurprisingly, therefore, we are not currently able to cure the condition and in most cases can only provide varying control of the signs and symptoms of the disease with powerful drugs which themselves often have un-pleasant side effects. However, this is better than the brain surgery that was administered to so many sufferers in the 1940s and 1950s (more on this in the next chapter).

The clinical manifestations of the disease are highly varied and it is clear that there are almost certainly a variety of forms of the disorder. Common symptoms are thought disorder, hallucinations, and thought insertion, all of which can disturb the patients' perception of reality. A considerably rarer symptom of the disease is the tendency for patients to report what appear to be forms of synaesthesia. I first encountered the occurrence of synaesthesia in psychosis when asked to review a book entitled *The Human Brain* for the *Times Higher Educational Supplement*. In this book the author briefly discusses synaesthesia and mentions that it is sometimes found in patients with psychosis. This comment intrigued Baron-Cohen and I, as we were unaware of any published accounts of synaesthesia in psychosis. Furthermore, when we canvassed the opinion of several psychiatrists they clearly stated that they were aware that accounts of mixed sensation were believed to be a possible symptom of psychosis, but that they personally had never encountered such a case. In fact, the only published study I can find that deals with synaesthesia in psychiatric disorder is a 1988 report entitled 'Synaesthesia and Major Affective Disorder'. This is a brief account of two cases of depression that appears to have given rise to forms of synaesthesia. Both cases are fairly short and I have therefore reproduced them in full:

Case 1

EM, a 42-year-old female with no past history of psychiatric symptoms, was admitted to the unit after childbirth with a sustained and morbid depressive change in her affect. On examination she was agitated, depressed, and weeping. She had delusions of bodily disease, and ideas of guilt and inadequacy concerning her care for her baby. She described anhedonia, anorexia, late insomnia, a diurnal rhythm to her symptoms, and poor concentration. She reported her senses as 'all mixed up', with varieties of synaesthesia. These were olfactory gustatory synaesthesia, as she could 'taste in the nose' and 'smell in the mouth', as well as auditory gustatory synaesthesia, during which she would 'hear my taste'. Physical investigations were unremarkable, and initial treatment with a tricyclic antidepressant and subsequently with electroplexy were ineffective. She later responded to phenelzine, with resolution of both the affective disturbance and the perceptual upset, and remains well 1 year later.

Case 2
MW, a 45-year-old female with no past history of psychiatric symptoms, was admitted to the unit following a suicide attempt. She complained of depression, irritability, fatigue, loss of libido, poor concentration, anorexia with significant weight loss, and early morning wakening. She described synaesthesia as she reported 'tasting' the 'pain' from her cervical spondylosis in her 'mouth'. Initially the patient made a partial recovery after electroplexy and thioridazine, with some improvement in mood but continuing synaesthesia, depressive cognitive set, and vegetative upset. Amitriptyline was introduced and, over the following weeks, there was a complete resolution of the affective and perceptual changes.

In both cases the synaesthesia seems to have been integral to the affective disorder as, in each instance, the condition resolved with successful antidepressant treatment. These two cases are interesting as in neither case do the patients appear to be deluded, and so one assumes that the accounts they give are of a genuine experience. We are not told whether the presence of synaesthesia was systematically tested. Most likely the patients were asked about signs and symptoms of their depression, at which point their synaesthesia symptoms were noted down and accepted at face value. Assuming that their synaesthesia was real, it is interesting to note that the forms (taste–smell, taste–hearing and taste–pain) of synaesthesia reported are very different to those experienced by the majority of idiopathic synaesthetes.

It is, of course, quite possible that psychiatrists rarely ask psychotic patients about this as a possible symptom and so its prevalence might be under-reported. However, even supposing that a patient with psychosis did inform us that they, for instance, saw colours when they heard sounds, what would we make of such a statement? A major difficulty with evaluating this claim would be distinguishing between at least three possible explanations: that the patient had in fact been hallucinating; that they were deluded about his experience; and, finally, that they had indeed experienced synaesthesiae in response to auditory stimulation. Our difficulty from a scientific perspective is that we currently have no way to pick between these various possibilities. However, it might be that functional imaging has the capacity to assist us in at least dissociating synaesthesia from hallucinations. You might recall Professor Frith's view that neuroimaging is a useful methodology for seeking to provide objective evidence of a subjective mental state? If we could scan psychotic patients who reported coloured hearing synaesthesia in the same paradigm as that used in the PET study and obtain similar patterns of activation, then we might have cause to suppose that these patients were indeed experiencing synaesthesiae. However, this would unfortunately not be conclusive, as certain forms of synaesthesia, even variants of coloured hearing, may have entirely different neural substrates, as may well be the case with synaesthesiae experienced as the result of drug abuse, which is considered next.

Synaesthesia in drug abuse

It is reasonably common for individuals who take hallucinogens to report that their senses become mixed. Given the illicit nature of the topic it is hard to find reliable data on this issue, but a recent web-based questionnaire conducted by Don DeGracia (http://www.csp.org/practices/entheogens/docs/kundalini_survey.html), suggested that, of a total of 62 respondents who admitted to using hallucinogenic compounds, 45.9% reported synaesthesic symptoms. Clearly the most common manifestation (over 90%) was to see sounds. Now, just as with the patients described in the last section, it would be prudent to treat such accounts with an element of caution, as it can be hard to dissociate 'true' synaesthesia from possibly imagined forms of the condition. Let us assume for the purposes of argument that substances such as hashish (see Chapter 5, The Usual Suspects, especially Baudelaire), LSD, and other hallucinogens really do evoke coloured hearing, does this tell us anything about idiopathic synaesthesia? We know very little about how substances such as LSD affect the brain, but the best evidence is that they probably work by interfering with the action of serotonin in neurons of the Raphé nuclei and the locus coeruleus (Figure 32).

Now, both of these areas are highly connected to a number of different brain regions, including targets in the cerebral

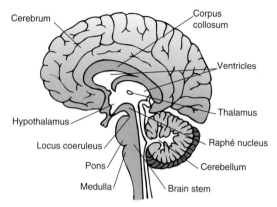

Figure 32 Locations within the brain of the Raphé nucleus and locus coeruleus.

cortex, and recent PET studies of the effect of LSD suggest that the areas typically activated are not those that lit up in our PET experiment. This suggests that the neural substrates of auditory visual events as a result of drug use are not the same as the substrates of idiopathic synaesthesia. In fact, it is not at all clear why we should expect any similarity; the subjective accounts given by hallucinogen users and synaesthetes are, after all, quite markedly different.

A number of the issues raised in the first half of this chapter are also important in our consideration of the theories proposed to explain synaesthesia. What should be clear from the variety of different forms of synaesthesia is that we should not necessarily expect one theory to explain all manifestations of the condition, though at least one commentator seeks to do so. In the next section, the various theories posited to account for the condition are described and discussed.

What causes synaesthesia?

Over the past two hundred years a number of hypotheses have been forwarded to explain the cause of synaesthesia. However, before discussing them it is worth pointing out Marks' dismissal of neurobiological accounts. His stance should be seen in the context of the time in which Marks was writing and, as is described in the following section, a number of recent findings suggest plausible neurobiological causes of the condition. Let's begin with what for us has been the null hypothesis explanation, that synaesthetes have unwittingly learned to associate words and sounds with colours.

1. Learned association

One of the earliest references to this theory was a paper by Calkins published in 1893. His view is that individuals who report seeing colours have unwittingly learned to associate colours with sounds and/or words. Thus for Calkins, as well as other commentators, there is simply a learned association, the origins of which the individual is unaware. The essence of this theory was well expressed by the eminent neurologist, Macdonald Critchley, who wrote that this theory:

> Subsumes that colour-synaesthesia is the product of a chain of mental associations, some of the intermediate links having dropped out of awareness. Thus the familiar story of trumpet blasts provoking a photism of red, may stem from the fact that such a sound immediately culls up in some persons an imagery of soldiers on parade. Ordinarily they shall be in dress uniform. This evokes a mental picture of scarlet. Should the middle part of this notion eventually become submerged, there will remain a synaesthetic linkage of trumpet-calls with redness.

Variations on this theme have been forwarded by other commentators, including some of the synaesthetes we have met. A popular explanation is that synaesthetes have been given coloured letter books as children and either consciously or unconsciously learned to associate letters with colours. Contrary to this notion is that synaesthetes are typically unable to recall having learned these specific colour associations. It is also revealing that for many synaesthetes consecutive letters are different shades of the same colour. This pattern of letter colours is untypical of the coloured alphabet books we have examined, which tend to make consecutive letters quite different colours from one another. It also follows that members of the same family should have been exposed to similar sources of letter–colour associations and so we should expect to see some similarity in the colour–letter correspondences reported by siblings, and mothers and daughters in the same family. However, we have found that their respective coloured alphabets tend to be very different even when the siblings have been twins. If a learned association explanation is sufficient to explain the condition, it is surprising that there is not greater similarity in the colour–letter correspondences within families. There are a number of other objections to explanation by simple association, including the fact that we have never met a synaesthete who is able to recollect *knowing* that their letter–colour associations were learnt either purposefully or incidentally. However, perhaps the most difficult issue to explain is the sex ratio of female to male synaesthetes. If all coloured hearing synaesthesia is explicable in the terms of learned association, then why would so many more women form such associations? It seems safe to conclude that the learned association theory of synaesthesia has not yet provided satisfactory explanations of these anomalies.

2. Sensory leakage theory

Studies of pseudosynaesthesia occurring in individuals with brain injury has often pressed authors into suggesting that photisms and synaesthesiae are because of leakage between senses. Variants of this theory could also, in principle, be used to explain idiopathic synaesthesia, so we will look in a little more detail at this theory.

With respect to coloured hearing synaesthesia, the essence of the theory is that auditory information 'leaks' into pathways and into areas in the brain that ordinarily deal with visual information. A number of different locations have been proposed as candidate sites where the plumbing might be leaky. Jacobs *et al.* suggested that one likely neural location for this leakage is the lateral geniculate nucleus, part of the thalamus, the 'telephone exchange of the brain'. However, Jacobs *et al.* concede that there are 'numerous regions of the brain where visual and auditory pathways lie in close anatomic proximity'. Other candidate regions would include the Raphé nucleus, implicated in drug-induced synaesthesia, and anterior visual pathways, as suggested by cases of optic nerve damage.

Evidence to support leakage between areas subserving different forms of sensory information is sparse, causing some difficulties for Jacobs *et al.*'s theory. However, recent work has suggested that, rather than posit the need for leakage, it is possible to find classes of neurons that are responsive to stimulation from more than one sensory modality at certain locations in the brain. For example, in a 1994 study carried out by Graziano *et al.*, recordings were made from more than 140 neurons in the ventral portion of the premotor cortex. Of these neurons, about 30% were found to be bimodally responsive, firing as a result of either, or both, visual and somasthetic stimulation.

The existence of bimodally responsive neurons means that other brain areas could produce ambiguous interpretations of the firing of these neurons. Presumably, under normal circumstances, areas that deal with afferent sensory information provide details of the *source* of these data. However, as Halligan *et al.* have recently suggested, when normal brain function is disrupted, access to other sources of information regarding the nature of these data might be lost. The patient DN reported by Halligan *et al.* might provide an example of this. As a result of brain damage causing hemianaesthesia, he is unable to feel tactile stimuli administered to his left side. However, when permitted to observe the application of the stimulus he reports tactile sensation. If Halligan's theory turns out to be an accurate account of DN's condition, then this provides an example of how the brain seeks to provide a meaningful interpretation of incoming sensory stimulation when deprived of a full complement of information. This notion might be familiar to you, especially from the earlier account of what might occur in dreaming as Halligan's patient also appears to be trying to make sense of incomplete or ambiguous information.

3. Cytowic's theory of synaesthesia

Perhaps the most controversial theoretical account of synaesthesia is that recently advanced by Cytowic (1993). He proposes that synaesthesia occurs because 'parts of the brain get disconnected from one another … causing the normal processes of the limbic system to be released, bared to consciousness, and experienced as synaesthesia' (p.163). An analogy is drawn with migraine, based upon the notion that, in both conditions, a stimulus causes a rebalancing of regional metabolism. Cytowic maps the analogy by pointing out that both synaesthesia and migraine (of some kinds) are evoked by a stimulus, and consequently, just as the migraine stimulus causes metabolic and circulatory changes, so too does the stimulus in synaesthesia. Cytowic's principal evidence for the involvement of the limbic system is the 'stunning shut-down of the cortex' observed in the xenon-133 studies of regional cerebral blood flow in MW's brain. Unfortunately, SPECT using xenon-133 does not permit deep brain structures such as the limbic system to be imaged. Direct evidence of the involvement of the limbic system would have been provided by evidence of blood flow changes in this brain region. Unfortunately, we have no imaging data on other polymodal synaesthetes of Cytowic's acquaintance. It would be interesting to know whether any of the other synaesthetes examined by Cytowic exhibit similar blood flow characteristics to those described for MW.

For Cytowic the impact of synaesthesia is so profound that, rather than fit current theories of brain function to data collected on synaesthetes, he suggests we should instead revise our theories of brain function to fit the data collected on synaesthetes. It is difficult not to have some sympathy for the view that current theories of brain function are probably inadequate. Nevertheless, there is no persuasive evidence to support Cytowic's radical new theory of how the brain operates.

4. Grossenbacher's theory

Back with more conventional neuroscience, another recent explanation has been proposed by Peter Grossenbacher and his colleagues. This theory was outlined in a recent article on synaesthesia published in *Discover* magazine in December 1999.

Grossenbacher has suggested that synaesthetes have unusually strong 'feed-backward' activity in their sensory pathways. He points out that the human brain is organized so that sensory input travels from cortical modules that deal with sense data from a single sensory domain into multi-sensory areas. These multisensory areas allow sense data from a variety of modalities to be combined so that tasks that require mapping sense data from one modality to data collected from another can be successfully executed (i.e. picking out by touch objects only previously seen). Grossenbacher also points out that these single and multimodal areas are reciprocally connected, though in most people the pathways leading from multimodal to unimodal areas are inhibited. In his view this inhibition can be reduced or extinguished, thereby giving rise to the experience of synaesthesia. Again, direct evidence for this theory is hard to come by, though Grossenbacher points out that the results of our PET study showed activation in multimodal areas. Grossenbacher also proposes that there is a logical contradiction in adopting the theory that synaesthesia is because of preserved neonatal pathways. He is quoted as saying that 'If you give people enough LSD or mescaline, they will often experience synesthesia … These people obviously aren't growing new connections in their brains. They're using connections we all have, but in a novel way'. However, this view presupposes that the neural substrates of idiopathic and drug-induced synaesthesia are the same, whereas the available evidence suggests that they are very different.

5. Environmentally shaped brain maturation

In the last chapter we encountered the notion of apoptosis, or programmed cell death. Set against this is cell death as the consequence of under use. The underlying issues regarding this theory of synaesthesia require a little explanation, which is provided in the next few sections.

A time to live, a time to die

In Chapter 1 the theory that synaesthesia is due to the presence in adults of neonatal pathways between auditory and visual areas of the brain was discussed. In Chapter 7 this was linked to the possibility that, because of genetic reasons, the normal process of apoptosis may not occur in synaesthetes. Consequently, the functional segregation of the senses that occurs in non-synaesthetes may lead to a breakdown in modularity in those with synaesthesia. This form of apoptosis would most likely be because of predetermined chemical signals built into the genetic sequence, i.e. the chief influence being the structure of the organism itself. Programmed cell death (PCD) is commonplace outside the brain. For example, during fetal development the fingers and toes form as a consequence of tissue between the digits self-destructing. During menstruation the inner lining of the uterus sloughs off as the consequence of PCD. However, it is also clear that cells will commit suicide if they receive insufficient stimulation from other cells. In the context of brain function this apparently paradoxical situation actually makes good sense and has influenced a number of theories of how the brain learns to process information, and potentially reconciles the two sides of the nature–nurture debate.

The violin-playing Nobel prize-winning neuroscientist

Professor Gerald Edelman (1929–) could have been a competent professional violinist but instead decided to devote his energies to clinical research. That he received the Nobel prize for medicine in 1972 suggests that he might have made a good decision. Interestingly, his Nobel Laureate was awarded for work he had carried out in immunology. Before Edelman's work in immunology it was popularly

supposed that infection, the invasion of our bodies by antigens, was met by a single type of specialist cells, lymphocytes, that sought out these invaders and fought them off.
The mystery was how a single cell could produce an
immune response to the vast array of different invaders.
Edelman's contribution was to show that rather than produce one flexible, single lymphocyte, the body in fact
randomly generates a huge range of millions of different
lymphocytes. When an invading organism provokes an
immune response these lymphocytes compete for the hon-
our of taking on the invader. The successful lymphocytes
are then selected and is produced by the body ready for the
next invasion.

There appears to be a strong tendency for scientists from
other disciplines to find themselves interested in brain
function, and Edelman is a good example of this tendency.
In his case interest in brain function appears to have been
because of his view that selection principles can be extended from immunology to the brain.

Neural Darwinism

Finding that a principle similar to natural selection was at
work in a microsystem such as our immune response
appears to have raised the possibility in Edelman's mind
that the new brain is born with the potential to develop in a
number of ways. Just as invading antigens select out the
most suited lymphocyte, so incoming sense data may select
out certain patterns of connectivity between neurons such
that these form small networks, with some surviving whilst
others are doomed to die. It is important to stress that
Edelman's view is so far unproven, though it does provide
an intuitively appealing account of how brain development
may occur. It may also reconcile the polarity of the nature–

nurture debate as, by Edelman's account, nurture sculpts the structure of a genetically determined organ. This perspective is also helpful in reminding us that a genetic predisposition is not necessarily a *fait accompli*; our phenotype is shaped by the interaction between our genotype and our experience. Neural Darwinism also helps to explain why such extensive PCD should occur in the young brain because, by this account, cells that receive significant input are selected for survival, whereas those that receive meagre input are destined to die. Recent research suggests that PCD is only part of the explanation. Evidence is accumulating to suggest that experience can have far reaching effects on brain structure–function relationships, as discussed in the next section.

Use it or lose it
There is now a vast amount of information to confirm that environmental factors shape brain structure through the selective reinforcement of specific neural connections. More Nobel prize-winning work, this time by David Hubel (1926–) and Torsten Wiesel (1924–), has shown that experience plays a major role in shaping the structure of the brain. Their work showed that different categories of cells in the visual cortices responded to specific shapes, sizes, colours, and line intensities. They also discovered that these cells pass information to cells that assembled these individual pieces of information into an image. To illustrate, one array of cells might respond only to a straight line with a specific angle. Yet other cell arrays would respond only to lines with a different angle. These line detection arrays are thus the building blocks for richer images in which groups of lines are conjoined to yield curves and arcs. It also seems that animals deprived of visual stimulation during certain

sensitive periods exhibit marked changes in areas of the visual cortex. The importance of this work for our consideration of the possible causes of synaesthesia is that it shows how early visual experience, acquired whilst the brain is relatively 'plastic', can have a lasting impact upon neural structure.

Synaesthetes' brains might therefore be 'shaped' by environmental factors. The circumstances by which this may occur are necessarily speculative, though recently Francis Crick has suggested a means by which this might occur. He suggests that individuals who in later life test positive for synaesthesia are those who have been given coloured letters to play with as neonates. The association between letters and colours becomes 'hardwired' into their brains so that later in life the occurrence of the letter is sufficient to evoke the colour.

This theory of synaesthesia superficially appears to share much in common with the learned associative theory discussed earlier. However, substantial differences exist. Both theories view synaesthesia as the consequence of environmentally mediated mechanisms, but these are not necessarily synonymous with one another. Learned associations do not necessarily require direct connections between auditory and visual areas of the brain. Associations of this kind are likely to be made at the level of semantics and therefore stored as engrams, possibly in areas of temporal cortex. By contrast, environmentally shaped pathways require direct connections between auditory and visual areas of the brain. Thus, whilst the association is stored in the brain, the areas that subserve learned associations are more memories of an event rather than hardwired direct connections between auditory and visual brain areas. Put slightly differently, the environmental shaping theory of synaesthesia suggests that within us all is the potential to remain a synaesthete, whereas the genetic theory suggests that only those biologically disposed to synaesthesia will develop the condition. This fascinating possibility, that with the right training we could all have florid synaesthesia, opens up the likelihood that one can experience synaesthesia in varying degrees and that we may all be synaesthetes, a prospect that will be considered in the next theory.

6. Is it quantitative or qualitative?

In most sciences debates occasionally arise as to whether certain events, objects, individuals, or diseases are clearly 'different' from the norm or whether they are simply different in degree. Differences of the first type are usually described as qualitative, whereas those of the second type are described as being quantitative. This debate also occurs in some commentators' accounts of synaesthesia. Many of these commentators point out that normal participants exhibit a willingness to make intersensory cross-modal matches, particularly between auditory and visual phenomena. Professor Lawrence Marks has conducted a number of these experiments and has shown that normal participants exhibit remarkable consistency in their ability to match a sound of 1000 Hz with the brightness of white light. He has also shown that they exhibit marked similarity in their ability to rate auditory visual metaphors using rating scales for loudness, pitch, and brightness. Marks observed remarkable consistency with regard to the judgements made, noting that just about everyone rated 'sunlight' as louder than 'glow', which was in turn rated louder than 'moonlight'.

Just as Marks has shown that auditory and visual judgements can interact with one another, so Zellner and Kautz, in 1990, reported that perceived odour intensity can be affected by the colour of a smelled substance. In their discussion Zellner and Kautz suggest that their effect may be due to conditioned association or that it might be 'the result of residual intersensory neural connections'. With respect to the first hypothesis, they point out that clear, colourless solutions are generally lacking in odour whereas coloured solutions can generally be expected to be aromatic. In fact, so strong is this expectation that participants in Zellner and Kautz's experiment who were asked to judge coloured and uncoloured solutions of equal odour intensity refused to believe the equality when debriefed. Their notion that the correspondence is because of direct connectivity obviously shares much in common with other theories of synaesthesia, including our own.

So, are individuals with synaesthesia fundamentally different in kind or simply just in degree? One possibility is that apparently non-synaesthesic individuals in fact have a mild form of the condition, i.e. just enough to be able to make the kind of cross-modal associations identified by Marks and by Zellner and Kautz. In medicine we use the term *forme fruste* (French for 'mild form') to describe a minimal form of a medical condition which is so mild that on casual inspection it escapes detection and thus diagnosis. One possibility then is that we all of us have a *forme fruste* of synaesthesia and are thus not qualitatively different from synaesthetes but merely quantitatively so. However, it is important to remember that research designed to test whether synaesthesia is found in all normal individuals shares some of the obstacles that exist in work with the profoundly synaesthesic. We cannot be sure that the willingness of normal participants to make similar judgements concerning the relationship between bright visual phenomena and high-pitched sounds is necessarily the result of learning culturally inherited metaphors or a mild form of synaesthesia.

A grand unifying theory?

Lawrence Marks suggested in his 1975 paper that the hypotheses posited as explanations 'for synaesthesia in all its sundry forms' seem insufficient. I would have to agree, but perhaps one reason for the confusion is the looseness with which synaesthesia is attached to various phenomena. For example, the term synaesthesia is currently used to describe the experiences of those who suffer photisms as a consequence of damage to visual pathways and individuals who hallucinate as a result of drug use. No single theory is likely to account for this variety of forms successfully. The term also creeps into use in circumstances where metaphor is likely to capture the nature of the phenomenon better. It also seems a priori very unlikely that we should expect an explanation of Cytowic's 'man who tasted shapes' synaesthesia to explain coloured hearing satisfactorily.

In the process of detailing the various theories of the cause of synaesthesia I came to realize that they are not necessarily mutually exclusive accounts. Implicit in most neuroscientific research is the idea that complete accounts of human behaviour require theories couched at both the functional and the structural level. Hence we return to the hierarchy of science that allows theories of the same concept to be phrased using sometimes very different vocabularies. Thus, these many apparently different theories do not so much compete as theoretical models of the condition as provide explanations couched in the vocabulary appropriate to the discipline.

CHAPTER 9

From romantic neurology to the ISA

In the last decade or so the synaesthesia story has come a long way, and many of the comments and claims made in the classical literature have been tested and largely found to be true. As a result of this renaissance of interest there are now several research groups around the world examining synaesthesia and related conditions. In this last chapter some of the work that is being carried out is discussed. Increased interest in the condition is valuable, as there is still a great deal about synaesthesia that requires explanation. In this final chapter some of the issues that require further investigation are summarized. Considerable text is devoted to one issue in particular, a solution for which even now eludes me after more than ten years of contemplation and research. It is simply this: what is it like to have synaesthesia? Before launching into these issues, let us take stock and summarize what we now know about the condition.

The story so far...

Before moving to a consideration of contemporary work on synaesthesia, I'll briefly review the experimental findings of the last eight chapters.

1. Synaesthetes are good at reproducing colour descriptions for words. We know for sure that they are better than control participants at this, even those who have been asked to try to remember simple word–colour pairings using mnemonic images.

2. Synaesthesia appears to run in families, just as Galton suspected, though in our experience it seems to be almost exclusively a female trait. The pedigrees collected to date suggest an X-linked dominant pattern of inheritance, perhaps with lethality in males. The condition appears to have a minimum prevalence of 1 in 2000.

3. Synaesthetes reliably affirm:
    a. They have always had the condition.
    b. That their colour–word correspondences are invariant.
    c. That they have tended not to discuss their synaesthesia with others for fear of ridicule.

4. Synaesthetes show marked increases in regional cerebral blood flow (rCBF) to brain areas known to be involved in the processing of colour information, even when blindfolded and therefore deprived of visual input.

5. In terms of cognitive test performance, lifestyle, occupation, and demography, individuals with synaesthesia appear otherwise unremarkable.

6. Certain 'simple' forms of synaesthesia can be acquired as the result of neurological or psychiatric illness. However, the vast majority of synaesthetes studied by us and by other research groups have been free of any brain disorder.

7. Simple synaesthesiae are also sometimes experienced by users of hallucinogenic substances such as LSD.

This is a quick summary of the findings of our group, but what of other researchers? As suggested in the introduction to this chapter, synaesthesia research is now being conducted by several groups. Recently, one of these groups has reported the findings of their experimentation using electroencephalography (EEG).

More electrophysiology

You may recall that Elizabeth Stewart-Jones had her electrical brain activity measured on her visit to the Institute of Psychiatry? The purpose of this assessment was to determine whether any abnormalities showed up on her EEG, a clinical use of the technology. However, electrophysiology can also be used for research purposes, and a group from Hanover has recently published a study of coloured letter processing in synaesthetes as compared to non-synaesthetes. They adopted the same 10–20 lead system shown in Figure 4 and presented participants with sequences of letters which they were asked to monitor for a specific letter or number. Participants were asked to respond to the letter or number targets by pressing a button. The Hanover group recorded from various brain sites, but were particularly interested in activations that might occur in the frontal lobes. One of the activation sites observed in our PET study was a region of the right prefrontal cortex. This activation was interpreted to be related to the attentional demands of having to deal with hearing words that also have colour characteristics. Put another way, it might be that synaesthetes have to deal with an extra visual dimension when processing words which requires them to concentrate harder. However, when we supposed that the prefrontal activation was indeed explicable in terms of attention this was a leap of faith. I would be the first to stress that this is a reasonable explanation, based on previously published evidence. However, we had no direct evidence in support of this assumption. One reason for this is that it is very hard to describe the exact role of the frontal lobes. We have reasonably satisfactory accounts of the role of most brain regions and, for the most part, we are relatively certain that much the same region subserves the same function in most individuals. However, we are much less certain of our ground with respect to the frontal lobes, even to the extent that we sometimes use the expression 'frontal' to describe patients with frontal lobe lesions while not being able to specify the exact cognitive deficits from which they suffer. The role of the frontal lobes in cognitive function could qualify as currently the most challenging issue for neuropsychology to address. In the following section some of these challenges are explored and the reasons why the frontal lobes have remained such an enigma are discussed.

What do the frontal lobes do?

Opinion is very much divided on the matter. Some surgeons have tended to suppose that their only function is to hold up your forehead. This view may stem from the experience of lesioning or removing the frontal lobes, the infamous lobotomy procedure. This operation, also known as prefrontal leucotomy, was popularized by the Portuguese neurologist Antonio Egaz Moniz, who introduced the procedure as a method of pacifying aggressive or violent behaviour. The procedure was so successful that, in 1949, Moniz was awarded the Nobel prize in physiology and medicine. However, at around this time clinicians began to notice that many patients who underwent the procedure became overly passive, sometimes becoming inactive and showing marked reductions in the use of their initiative.

The lobotomy procedure was 'refined' to cutting nerve fibre bundles to the frontal lobes in the late 1940s. What remains extraordinary about the procedure is the relatively mild impact that it seemed to have upon behaviour and intellect. Unfortunately, little formal assessment of the impact of lobotomy was carried out and so it is hard to know whether the procedure was ever cognitively benign. In fact, we now know that such a procedure is likely to have compromised several cognitive skills whose neural substrates lie in the frontal lobes. The accidental discovery of antipsychotic drugs during the 1950s meant that this form of psychosurgery fell from favour as a method of managing patients.

The specific functions of the frontal lobes continue to confound the best efforts of neuroscience. The difficulty is that apparently similar frontal lobe lesions in two different individuals can have wildly varying impacts on their cognitive function. The variation is so substantial that sometimes small, seemingly insignificant lesions can cause huge psychological impairment, whereas the loss of an entire frontal lobe sometimes has no, or only minor, cognitive implications. An excellent case of major behavioural change after frontal lobe lesion is the story of Phineas Gage, possibly neurosciences' best known case history.

Don't touch that...

Phineas Gage was the foreman of a railway construction gang working on the Rutland & Burlington railway and, by all accounts, a very smart, intelligent man with a reputation for being a model employee. Unfortunately for Phineas, on the 13th September 1848 he was setting a tamping iron

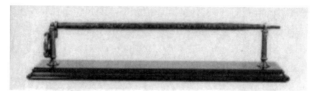

Figure 33 Tamping iron exhibit. The tamping iron that was blown through Phineas Gage's head. The iron was 3 feet 7 inches long, weighed 13.5 pounds, and was 1.25 inches in diameter at one end, tapering over a distance of about 1 foot to a diameter of 0.25 inch at the other.

(Figure 33) when the charge he had placed accidentally exploded and blew the bar through his head.

The sketch of Gage's skull (Figure 34) made by the physician who attended him, Dr John Harlow (1819–1907), gives a good impression of the substantial damage done to Gage's brain. Remarkably, it seems that Gage may not even have lost consciousness as a result of the accident, even though the tamping iron appears to have entered the underside of his left cheek, destroyed the left frontal region of his brain and then exited the top of his head with sufficient force to travel a further 30 yards.

Some time later Phineas felt physically well enough to return to his job as foreman. Unfortunately, he was deemed by his employers to be no longer capable of carrying out his duties, not because of a catastrophic reduction in cognitive skills, but because he had undergone marked personality changes. It seems the brain injury had caused Phineas to become an irreverent and profane individual who had also become impatient and obstinate and apparently unable to follow projects though to completion. He was, as friends commented, no longer Gage. The case of Phineas Gage tempts one into supposing that damage to the left pre-

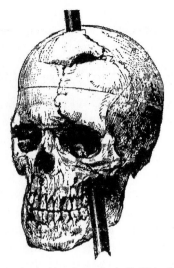

Figure 34 Harlow's sketch of Gage's skull. This sketch, made by Dr John Harlow, Gage's physician, shows the trajectory of the tamping iron shown in Figure 33 through Gage's skull.

frontal lobe should reliably cause personality change. Unfortunately, this is not always the case; often patients can undergo substantial frontal lobe removal and yet apparently suffer very few ill effects. Yet in others an apparently minute lesion can cause wholesale cognitive dysfunction.

But do you need your frontal lobes?

During my time in neuroscience I have encountered various pieces of evidence to suggest that localization of function becomes more difficult to demonstrate the further forward one travels in the brain. For example, lesions in the occipital lobes tend to have fairly predictable cognitive consequences. In contrast, lesions to frontal lobe locations have considerably less predictable consequences for cognitive function. I shall always remember my first 'frontal lobe' patient, a very pleasant 30-year-old woman from Birmingham who had the misfortune to suffer a slow growing tumour that impacted her frontal lobe. She had neurosurgery to remedy this and had the foremost 5.5 cm of her left frontal lobe removed. The operation was a success and I arranged to conduct a thorough neuropsychological assessment three days after her operation. In preparation I assembled a prodigious array of tests previously shown to be sensitive to frontal lesions, and tested her for a good couple of hours, with occasional breaks. Amazingly, she turned in a robust performance on every test, not once straying outside the normal range! I was somewhat astonished, but further work on the frontal lobes has confirmed the observation that some patients with frontal lobe damage suffer profound changes in cognitive function*. Whilst others, in spite of suffering extensive frontal lobe injury, apparently escape any cognitive disability.

---

* My failure to find any evidence of cognitive dysfunction in this lady was a great surprise. Perhaps you are thinking 'now wouldn't that make an interesting report?' Well, on the face of it, yes, but a sad fact of life in neuroscience is that 'null' findings are deemed to be of little interest to journals, so one is 'brought up' to believe that studies that show no effects are uninteresting and therefore unworthy of publication. In fact, such findings are often even described as negative findings. The reluctance of authors to submit null findings may have led to the establishment of a very biased literature. Remember that we adopt the 5% level of significance for our statistical tests? This adoption means that, if one conducted the same experiment 20 times, then by chance rather than as the result of a genuine real effect, one would get a statistically significant effect. Such a result would be what statisticians call a type 2 error. This scenario has been described as the file drawer problem in recognition that many interesting and important studies may have been consigned to the file drawer rather than sent to journals for publication.

One possible reason for the variable impact of frontal lobe lesions upon cognition might be because of the strategies adopted by different individuals in negotiating so-called frontal lobe tests. For example, one popular view of frontal lobe function is that these areas are recruited when the problem to be solved is novel. By this rationale a test will be sensitive to frontal lobe damage only if the task is new to the patient. The performance of my first ever frontal lobe patient, who confessed a lifelong interest in puzzles and games (which sometimes bore marked similarities to some of the tests I gave her), might be a good example of this. One excellent example of this was the selection of a task known as the Stockings of Cambridge. This test is a variant of the famous Tower of London problem, shown in Figure 35.

My patient had absolutely no problem with this task, in spite of its reputation as a robust test of what are classically regarded as frontal lobe functions, such as planning, strategy, and the capacity to inhibit responses. However, and as noted, she spontaneously mentioned that she had previously encountered, and solved, similar problems as those that comprise the Tower of London game.

Hanover revisited

The foregoing comments suggest that we should be very cautious in the interpretation of the increased rCBF seen in the PET study, or the different EEG activity seen in the Hanover group's study. However, there are other issues to consider regarding the Hanover study. The synaesthetes in the Hanover study were asked to monitor (i.e. read) letters or numbers and to respond to targets by pressing a response key. This highlights a crucial difference between the synaesthetes we have tested and those selected by the Hanover

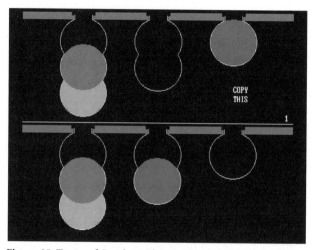

Figure 35 Tower of London. The Tower of London (sometimes referred to as the Tower of Brahma or the End of the World Puzzle) was invented by the French mathematician, Edouard Lucas, in 1883. He was inspired by a legend that tells of a Hindu temple where the pyramid puzzle was used for the mental discipline of young priests. Legend says that, at the beginning of time, the priests in the temple were given a stack of 64 gold disks, each one a little smaller than the one beneath it. Their assignment was to transfer the 64 disks from one of the three poles to another, with one important proviso – a large disk could never be placed on top of a smaller one. When they finished their work, the myth said, the temple would crumble into dust and the world would vanish. In the example illustrated, the subject's task is: 'to make the bottom of the screen look like the top' by moving balls in the bottom half. This is an example of a one-move problem; all that is needed is to move the ball in the central pocket to the far right pocket. See also Plate 3. Reproduced with permission of CeNeS Pharmaceuticals.

group. We have consistently found that it is necessary for the synaesthetes we have tested to hear words and letters for their synaesthesiae to be elicited. It is not entirely clear from the Hanover group's study, but the presumption one makes is that for their synaesthetes it was sufficient for them to read the letters. Thus, in spite of showing apparently similar brain region activity, it might be that these two groups manifest qualitatively different forms of the condition.

What is it like to have synaesthesia?

You might recall from discussions in Chapter 4 that, in spite of more than a decade of work and contemplation, I still didn't feel that I had a good understanding of what it is like to have synaesthesia. In the intervening chapters nothing much has changed, but we should perhaps dwell on what it might be like and whether it is ever possible for non-synaesthetes to understand what it is like. One of the most evocative accounts of what it is to have synaesthesia is Alison Motluk's wonderful account of her weekend spent with Elizabeth. Alison, currently a journalist working for *New Scientist*, is a synaesthete herself and was able, in her chapter ('Two synaesthetes talking colour') in *Synaesthesia: Classic and Contemporary Readings*, to convey as good an impression of what it is to have synaesthesia as I have ever encountered. Alison also makes clear that, while both she and Elizabeth would be described as synaesthetes, differences between them exist. Alison has the form typical of those participants reported in Chapter 3, 'the more common and constrained' whereas she describes Elizabeth's synaesthesia as being 'more precise, detailed and distinctive'. Later in the chapter she illustrates the differences thus:

> If there is such a thing as word-envy, I have it now. These are not, I realize, with some defeat, very much like the rather simple colours I attach to letters and words. Mine are all smoother, with a touch of shine here, velvet there, but overall rather flat and ordinary. 'Meredith' for me, for

instance, is a kind of flat grass green. But for Elizabeth it is a virtual tartan of colour; deep greens and purples intertwine and rise from the canvas. I can't help thinking how lovely a 'Meredith' wool jumper would be.

So, based on Alison's account, can we be sure that Elizabeth and she share a similar experience? Frankly no, the problem with other minds is that we cannot be sure that any two individuals genuinely understand the perspective and experience of one another.

Philosophical assistance

Earlier, I recounted how my experience of seeing things is restricted to data received as light on my retina, my 'mind's eye', or to visual events such as seeing stars. I further mentioned that synaesthetes reliably report that they too experience all these forms of visual event, but that their synaesthesiae are not like any of them. Given this, can I ever expect to understand what it is like to be a synaesthete? Richard Cytowic is fairly clear that, in his view, the only way to understand is to experience it first hand. He describes synaesthesia as noetic and ineffable, and therefore not comprehendable by non-synaesthetes. You won't be surprised to find that this is a familiar issue in neuroscience; in fact, it is simply a variant of a deep philosophical issue broadly known as the problem of other minds. So, what is the essence of this profound philosophical issue? Well, the first thing to say is that it is an issue that neatly divides neuroscience, not into two groups as is usually the case (nativists versus empiricists, etc.) but into many disparate groups. One perspective on this issue was provided by the philosopher Thomas Nagel. In this article, published in the *Philosophical Review*, Nagel asks 'What is it like to be a bat?' a question that forms the title and topic of his article. As Nagel says in his discussion, he could just as easily have asked what it is like to be a wasp or flounder. His reason for picking bats over these other species is simply that he felt that insects and fish were a little too far down the phylogenetic scale, whereas bats were sufficiently close to us to make his point. In the following section there is a brief introduction to Nagel's argument but, in advance of this, let me beg a small request. Nagel's account asks the reader to imagine what it is like to be a bat, but you might find it entertaining to substitute the word bat for synaesthete. Nagel also cites a statement that will ring several bells regarding the nature of scarlet.

What is it like to be a synaesthete?

Nagel's article is in fact a consideration of another famous philosophical problem for neuroscience, the 'mind–body problem'. This is a variant of issues we met earlier, specifically what is the mind and how does it interact with the body? The essential issue for Nagel is how can we provide a satisfactory explanation of our own conscious experience, a personal and subjective phenomenon? Nagel's starting assumption is that the question we are asking is what is it like to be another organism because, if we can imagine what it is like, then that other organism is likely to have conscious experience. Nagel picks bats for consideration simply because bats perceive the world in ways very different from our own, tending to use sonar or echolocation for tasks for which we tend to use vision. His challenge is simply this, can we ever understand what it is like to be a bat? Nagel characterizes the difficulty thus:

> Our own experience provides the basic material for our imagination, whose range is therefore limited. It will not

help to try to imagine that one has webbing on one's arms, which enables one to fly around at dusk and dawn catching insects in one's mouth; that one has very poor vision; and perceives the surrounding world by a system of reflected high-frequency sound signals; and that one spends the day hanging upside down by one's feet in an attic. In so far as I can imagine this (which is not very far), it tells me only what it would be like for me to behave as a bat behaves. But that is not the question. I want to know what it is like for a bat to be a bat. Yet if I try to imagine this, I am restricted to the resources of my own mind, and those resources are inadequate to the task. I cannot perform it either by imagining additions to my present experience, or by imagining segments gradually subtracted from it, or by imagining some combination of additions, subtractions and modifications.

Nagel is clear on this; while we can *imagine* what it is like to be a bat, *knowing* what it is to be a bat presents substantial challenges. We can develop a subjective view fairly readily, but an objective view is rather more difficult to achieve. I have come to the view that my desire to understand what it is to be a synaesthete presents similar challenges. I can imagine what it is like to be a synaesthete, but knowing what it is like is a struggle, just as knowing what it is like to move around the world using echolocation presents a challenge. So challenging is this reconciliation of the subjective experience (imagining) with the objective (knowing) that some commentators have concluded that the gap is unbridgeable and that an explanation will always evade us. My physicalist philosophy forbids such nihilistic thinking, though this issue presents a significant challenge to my adherence to physicalism. Nagel, however is optimistic about bridging this gap and closes his essay with 'a speculative proposal'. He suggests that one possible solution is to develop an objective phenomenology, a language that would allow us to understand the experience of other organisms without reference to imagination. Nagel acknowledges that this constitutes quite a challenge and suggests that, rather than beginning by trying to understand what it is to be a bat, we should instead begin by trying to understand what it is to be another person. This is something we do as individuals every day. Huge portions of our behaviour rely upon being able to take the perspective of another, and considerable evidence has accrued to suggest that, as very young children, we develop a 'theory of mind' that facilitates our understanding of other people's perspectives. However, Nagel is looking for a little more than empathy, he is advocating a system that facilitates genuine understanding. This is clearly a tall order and, as Nagel proposed this approach as long ago as 1974 and as yet we have no significant progress, it might simply be that such an approach is untenable. We will stick with Nagel's view a little longer, as he uses what, for us, is an interesting quote.

Locke's blind truthseeker revisited

We discussed in Chapter 2 the case of the blind man who decided that 'he now knew what scarlet was like, it was like the sound of a trumpet'. I have always been unconvinced that this was indeed a genuine case of synaesthesia. Coincidentally, in the last paragraph of Nagel's bat essay he alludes to this case and dismisses it as a loose intermodal analogy. I couldn't have put it better myself; however, the context in which he raises this issue holds considerable interest for us. This quote is made in the context of Nagel's suggestion that, in seeking to develop an understanding of what it is to be something (bat, synaesthete, etc.), a good starting place would be to 'develop concepts that could be used to explain to a person blind from birth what it was like to see', perhaps beginning with an objective description of the structural features of perception. This is no trivial task, but if we truly wish to obtain an objective understanding of other people's (and bats') experience, a necessary one. I'd like to suggest something else as a means of furthering our understanding of what it is to be a synaesthete and also an understanding of the condition itself.

In Chapter 2 we found that there appeared to be high prevalence rates of synaesthesia amongst those who became blind as young children, but not in those blind from birth. The prevalence rate in this study was substantially higher than one would normally expect (we determined that synaesthesia is found in about one in every 2000 individuals). This suggests that a useful group of participants to work with are those who become blind in infancy. Of course we have no guarantee that their synaesthesia will be comparable to those we have studied as, in the blind group, synaesthesia will have been acquired rather than inherited. In fact, the limited evidence we have suggests that acquired cases will be less complex than the inherited form, as illustrated by the case of coloured tones reported by the retrolental fibroplasia sufferer discussed in the last chapter. Nevertheless, it is tempting to try to use this model as a means of illuminating our understanding, especially in light of recent neuroimaging work with blind participants.

Reorganization of brain function

One reason that brain damage is so debilitating is the inability of brain cells to regenerate themselves. Sadly, once a brain cell is lost it is lost forever. This is why strokes can have such devastating effects. However, sometimes substantial areas of brain are lost with relatively little loss of function. A good illustration of this is the example of individuals who undergo hemispherectomy, a dramatic surgical intervention in which one hemisphere of the brain is removed, usually as a remedy for intractable epilepsy. As we have seen, language tends to depend on neural structures in the left hemisphere and so a full, left hemispherectomy should deprive the patient of language skills. However, in almost all cases the patient successfully develops language function. Evidence suggests that this is because structures in the right hemisphere take on the task. If this degree of flexibility, or plasticity, as neuroscientists call it, exists with respect to brain function, why is it that stroke sufferers so often lose their ability to produce and/or comprehend speech? The reason for this variance between stroke and hemispherectomy patients would seem to be accounted for by age. Strokes, by and large, tend to occur in older individuals, whereas hemispherectomy tends to be carried out in infants. It seems that younger brains are more plastic than older ones, and that puberty is a critical period that coincides with the near completion of the myelination process discussed in Chapter 1.

There is extremely good evidence that the brain can adapt to injury, at least early in life. Of course the hemispherectomy example illustrates what can happen when brain territory is lost, but what about when input to the brain is diminished or lost? For example, what reorganizational changes take place when visual input via the eye is reduced or removed? Until recently it was simply impossible to address this issue. However, the advent of functional neuroimaging has recently provided us with the opportunity to study visually impoverished brains. An area of particular interest has been to examine which brain areas are activated when blind participants read braille. We know that the sensorimotor strip is the brain region that detects touch, so this would seem to be an obvious and expected neural substrate for braille reading. However, the research groups who undertook this work had some surprises in store, as will be described shortly.

See me, feel me

At a functional level we have become very inventive about finding alternative strategies for dealing with the loss of sensory information. Spectacles are an obvious example, as is the system of reading by touch invented by Louis Braille (1809–1852). Braille became blind as the result of an accident in which one of his father's shoemaking awls penetrated his eye. This injury soon became infected and, when the infection spread to young Louis' other eye, he became completely blind at the age of 3 years. Louis was a bright and ambitious chap and was enrolled at the National Institute for the Blind. During Braille's time at the Institute a French army captain, Charles Barbier de la Serre, visited the school to present the invention he called 'Night Writing'. This system was designed to provide soldiers with the means to communicate at night without speaking. De la Serre's system worked by representing sounds on a matrix of 12 dots. The system never saw military service and so Barbier de la Serre sought to adapt the system for use by the blind. Louis perceived that the 12-dot system was unnecessarily complex and that a six-dot system could function perfectly well as a means of representing the standard alphabet. A six-dot system also had the advantage that individual characters could be perceived with a single touch.

Braille reading is a relatively new human skill, just a couple of hundred years old. In terms of the history of our species, visual reading is also relatively new, being no more than a few thousand years old. Given this, it is unlikely that the human brain is specialized for reading. There simply hasn't been enough time for this to occur. Our ability to read is therefore likely to be subserved by a number of pre-existing cognitive skills, such as our ability to see and our language capacity, abilities we know are housed in occipital and temporal lobe structures. Much of our understanding of brain function has been revealed to us through nature's exceptions and, as a consequence, neuroscience has been much occupied with the various deficits exhibited by patients with physical damage to either the brain or the sense regions that convey information to the brain. The advent of functional neuroimaging has meant that, for the first time, we can look to see how nature deals with these exceptions. Individuals with congenital and acquired forms of blindness who have learned braille provide us with an excellent opportunity to see how the brain deals with the shift from visual to tactile forms of writing comprehension. The results have proven interesting, as we shall now see.

Imaging the neural substrates of touch

One of the first studies to be conducted in this area (Sadato *et al.* 1996) compared the blood flow maps of normal controls with those of braille readers who had been blinded early in life. All subjects were scanned while engaged in a tactile discrimination task and a tactile task that required no discrimination. As predicted the latter task yielded no unexpected activation in either group. However, a marked dissociation was seen in the discrimination task such that blood flow to primary visual areas *increased* in the braille readers group but *decreased* in normal subjects. This remarkable study has shown that brain regions ordinarily subserving vision are recruited when the unsighted are engaged in making tactile discriminations. As the authors state: 'in blind subjects, cortical areas normally reserved for vision may be activated by other sensory modalities' and that 'these findings suggest that the tactile processing pathways usually linked in the secondary somatosensory area are rerouted in blind subjects to the ventral occipital cortical regions originally reserved for visual shape discrimination'.

This study showed that the brains of those blinded in infancy were capable of recruiting in new brain areas when engaged in tasks requiring tactile discriminations. An obvious question to address is whether this effect holds true for those who never had vision, the congenitally blind. A second question to answer was whether the effects seen in the first study would hold true if study participants were engaged in reading braille, a more difficult task than the simple tactile discrimination utilized by Sadato *et al.*, and then to compare brain activation for braille reading with listening to speech. Some of our co-authors from the PET paper participated in the running of a study that sought to address these questions. They found that congenitally blind participants showed greater activation of extrastriate visual areas when reading braille compared to listening to speech. The other group of participants, selected on the basis that they retained their sight until after puberty, showed additional activation in primary visual areas.

Thus, it seems that the brains of blind braille readers use 'visual' cortices to aid the processing of tactile information. Perhaps, then, it is reasonable to suppose that visual areas in the brains of blind people may also become the substrates of auditory information. If so, this might begin to explain why the incidence of coloured-hearing synaesthesia has been observed to be as high as 50% in those who become blind in childhood. Starr (1893) might well have been wise to speculate that 'The colour-sound and mental imagery of the blind is, I am convinced, an interesting special field of study'. Perhaps future research will better inform us.

The view from Mother Russia

One of the saddest, and most artificial, divisions in modern life is that between art and science. The novelist CP Snow pleaded for a reconciliation between the two, but the gulf still seems irreconcilably wide. Odd really, having a foot in both camps didn't seem to hold back Leonardo da Vinci, but still it seems hard to be comfortable in both. Every year I give a plenary lecture at the Cambridge Art History summer school, a particular pleasure that allows me to hop between the two cultures, with, as usual, synaesthesia as my theme. Simon Baron-Cohen and I have, on occasion, been asked to write reviews on synaesthesia for arts journals and several years ago we wrote an article for the journal *Leonardo*, summarizing what was known about synaesthesia. A result of this article was a letter from a Russian researcher, Bulat Galeyev, an individual working at the Prometheus Institute in Georgia, with more than 40 years' experience of working on the condition. He provided a very different perspective on the condition for us.

To begin with, Galeyev denies that synaesthesia is a 'biological' function, instead supposing that it arises as a social and cultural phenomenon, more specifically as a 'manifestation of non-verbal thinking, realized by either involuntary or purposeful comparison of the impressions of different modalities'. A very different interpretation then, but could it fit with our experimental results? It could well fit with the brain imaging data, as the differences we saw between synaesthetes and non-synaesthetes may have simply been images reflecting differences in 'thinking'. So, what of the consistency of colour–word correspondence that we observe? Galeyev declares himself to be firmly in the learned association camp, suggesting that one should suppose conditioning 'by basic, psychological phenomenon ('intersensorial links')'.

He is clear in expressing his view that synaesthesia has no claim to the status of an unusual biological phenomenon. He is, in fact, quite damning in his critique of those who suggest that synaesthesia is an abnormal state, at one point describing his countryman Luria's (1966) description of S's synaesthesia as evidence that he was 'a victim of prejudice and author of evident nonsense'! For Galeyev synaesthesia is best described as being a 'co-imagination or co-feeling' and that 'by its psychological nature it is association, specifically intersensory association'. Thus it is his view that there is nothing special about the condition for, by his explanation we have, all of us, the capacity to experience synaesthesia. It is, as he claims 'The ability to connect in consciousness the visual and audible phenomena … inherent to everyone'.

Galeyev shares my sentiments about the oft-suggested synaesthesic status of Scriabin, Kandinsky, and others, clearly stating that they did not actually see colours. However, his reason for stating this is his fundamental belief that no synaesthete *actually* sees colours! So, is any reconciliation of Bulat M. Galeyev's view of synaesthesia with those of other commentators (including my own) possible? In this next, and final, section of the book I'll try to do this by suggesting a theoretical alternative to the accounts so far given, an account that, to use a phrase often heard on *Blue Peter*, you can all try at home.

Final thoughts

Of course, Galeyev's account of synaesthesia provides no explanation for the anomalies that litter our data, especially with reference to the sex ratio. It might also be, as suggested previously, that the phenomenon we are seeking to explain is qualitatively different to that being explained by Richard Cytowic, Bulat Galeyev, and others. However, the major challenge for me is to explain and thus understand the fundamental nature of the experience. After all, and apparently entirely contrary to Galeyev's view, the synaesthetes of our acquaintance carry the very strong conviction that they really do see colours. Nevertheless, I remain struck by the possibility that synaesthesia may be learnt by co-imagination or co-feeling, as Galeyev expresses it. I'd therefore like to suggest an experiment we can all try but, before doing so, let me discuss with you the background to these thoughts.

Eye witness testimony

In a famous series of experiments Professor Elizabeth Loftus discovered that, through subtle suggestive techniques, it was possible to influence a person's memory of an event. In an experiment carried out in 1974, she and a fellow researcher asked participants to watch a film of a multiple car accident, after which they asked the participants a number of questions about the clip. The independent variable in this experiment was the form of particular questions that participants were asked. One group was asked: 'About how fast were the cars going when they smashed into each other?'. Another group had the same question but the words 'smashed into' were substituted with 'hit'. A third group, the control group, were not asked a question about the speed of the cars. Participants were interviewed again 1 week later. Among the questions was one asking: 'Did you see any broken glass?'. Control participants and those receiving the 'hit' form of the question falsely recalled seeing glass in about 14% of cases. In contrast, 32% of the participants receiving the 'smashed into' version now recalled seeing broken glass, when in fact there was none. So, why did they fib? Well, perhaps accusing them of fibbing is a bit strong; it would be more appropriate to comment that they were misled into recollecting something that wasn't in fact there, namely the broken glass.

So, we know that at least some individuals can be induced to reconstruct a memory but can, by definition, have no recollection of originally encoding the event. Human experience of dreams, photisms, hallucinations, etc., all testify to the fact that our memories and perceptions can be influenced in ways not always accessible to consciousness. This could have relevance for our understanding of synaesthesia. A possibility does suggest itself – maybe we could train ourselves to have a kind of synaesthesia.

Let's suppose that we sat down and learnt to associate a few words with specific patterns of colour. Take, for example, the figures shown on the cover of this book, Elizabeth's 'portraits' of Alan Ayckbourne and Harold Pinter. Imagine the names of these playwrights as you gaze at the images. I have tried this over a protracted period of time (at the time of writing for about 6 months), and I have found that the mere mention of either name is now enough to bring the images vividly to consciousness. The experience is not like the mind's eye; for that experience I need to conjure the image, whereas in the case of Pinter and Ayckbourne the vision is immediate. While I know that the image is contrived (it is, after all, my contrivance), my certainty that I am not really seeing the image has reduced markedly over the last 6 months. This kind of introspective, transparent self-testing is a dangerous scientific enterprise. However, I am convinced that, through repetition of an event, the engram has become so ingrained in my mind that it starts to become as visually real as the broken glass 'remembered' by Loftus' participants. You might choose to try this 'experiment' on yourselves, now that you have reached the end of my account.

All good things

It is always tempting to keep on writing, but I think I've probably taken this topic as far as I reasonably might. I am a little afraid that I haven't provided as many answers as you would have liked but, then, we should be suitably modest about our achievements to date in the field of neuroscience. We have indeed made considerable progress in our understanding of mental phenomena in the last two decades, but we clearly have a long way to go before we can reasonably claim a genuine understanding of human behaviour, its cognitive underpinnings, and its neural basis. It is my belief that an explanation of synaesthesia is inherently important. It may turn out that the condition can be accounted for by simple learning theory, but I am not so sure. If this does turn out to be the case, even such an apparently mundane explanation has the capacity better to inform our understanding of cognition, behaviour, and brain function.

The most important thing for me is that you have enjoyed this book. I hope this has been the case. Thanks for reading.

Glossary

AC–PC line A line used as a reference point in mapping the human brain, obtained by connecting the anterior and posterior commissures (see Figure 15).

AEP Auditorily evoked potential.

Acalculia Loss of the ability to carry out mental arithmetic.

Achromatopsia Loss of the ability to perceive colour.

Agnosia Inability to recognize objects.

Agraphia Loss of the ability to write.

Akinetopsia Inability to perceive motion visually.

Allele One of the variant forms of a gene at a particular locus, or location, on a chromosome. Different alleles produce variation in inherited characteristics, such as hair colour or blood type. In an individual, one form of the allele (the dominant one) may be expressed more than another form (the recessive one).

Anatomy The study of the physical structure of the body.

Angular gyrus A brain 'ridge', damage to which is believed to cause Gerstmann's syndrome.

Aphasia Loss of speech.

Apoptosis Programmed cell death.

Autosome Any chromosome other than a sex chromosome.

BOLD Blood oxygenation level dependent. A technique for examining brain activity *in vivo*.

Behaviourism Psychological paradigm characterized by an adherence to dealing with observable behaviour.

Between design An experimental methodology by which different groups are evaluated.

Biochemistry The study of chemical reactions occurring in living organisms.

Biometry The measurement of the observable characteristics of living organisms.

Bradykinesia Poverty of movement, one of the cardinal signs of Parkinson's disease.

Broca's area Anatomically, the third convolution of the left frontal lobe, hypothesized by Paul Broca to be the neural substrate of speech production.

CAT Computerized axial tomography, now just CT.

Codon Three bases in a DNA or RNA sequence which specify a single amino acid.

Cognitivism The psychological paradigm whose focus of study is the mind.

Confounding variable Any variable that compromises our explanation of the IV's effect.

DLPFC Dorsolateral prefrontal cortex (see Figure 16).

Dependent variable The experimental variable that is measured.

Dominant A gene that almost always results in a specific physical characteristic; for example, a disease, even though the patient's genome possesses only one copy. With a dominant gene, the chance of passing on the gene to children is 50–50 in each pregnancy.

Dyschromatopsia A partial loss of the ability to perceive colour.

EPI Echo planar imaging.

EEG Electroencephalography

Electroencephalography See EEG

Electron Elementary particles that orbit the nucleus of atoms.

Empiricism Philosophical paradigm in which followers suppose that all knowledge is derived from experience.

Epilepsy Brain disorder characterized by the presence of abnormal electrical discharges occurring and causing seizures.

Exon The region of a gene that contains the code for producing the gene's protein. Each exon codes for a specific portion of the complete protein.

fMRI Functional magnetic resonance imaging.

Gene The functional and physical unit of heredity passed from parent to offspring. Genes are pieces of DNA, and most genes contain the information for making a specific protein.

Genome The DNA contained in an organism or a cell; this includes both the chromosomes within the nucleus and the DNA in mitochondria.

Gerstmann syndrome Neurological disorder characterized by difficulties with mental arithmetic.

Gesamtkunstwerk German term meaning 'total art work'.

Grundstorung German term roughly translating as 'general factor'.

Gustatory Pertaining to the sense of taste.

Haiku Japanese poetic form in 17 syllables.

Heterozygous Possessing two different forms of a particular gene, one inherited from each parent.

Homozygous Possessing two identical forms of a particular gene, one inherited from each parent.

Hypnopompia State between sleep and waking.

Hypnogogia State between waking and sleep.

Imaginal Of the imagination.

Independent variable Experimental variable under the control of the investigator.

In silico Experimentation conducted by computer.

Intron Regions of DNA that have no apparent function. Sometimes also called 'junk DNA'.

In utero In the uterus.

In vivo Experiment conducted in the living body.

In vitro Experiment conducted outside the body.

Ischaemia The inadequate supply of blood.

Kabuki Highly stylized form of Japanese theatre.

LGN The lateral geniculate nucleus (see Figure 11).

Localizationism In neuroscience, the view that cognitive functions can be tied to specific neural substrates.

MRI Magnetic resonance imaging.

Mnemonist Individual with prodigious memory skills.

Modularity View of human brain function which holds that cognition can be decomposed into a set of cohesive and loosely coupled skills.

Myelin Fatty tissue surrounding nerve cells and acting as an insulator.

NMR Nuclear magnetic resonance.

Nativism Philosophical paradigm popular with those who believe that many of our skills are innate.

Neurasthenia Tiredness or exhaustion, often in excess of what would seem appropriate from purely physical causes.

Neuron Cell specialized to convey electrochemical information.

Neuropsychology A branch of psychology concerned with the consequences of brain injury for cognitive function.

Neuroscience The study of the structure and function of the brain.

PET Positron emission tomography.

PGO Pons geniculate occipital.

Perinatal In the period either shortly before or after birth.

Phosphene A visual event, typically 'star-like' caused by pressure on the eyeball, optic damage, etc.

Phrenology Pseudoscience whose central dogma is that mental faculties are highly localized and can be determined from the size of the skull overlying these areas.

Physicalism Philosophy that supposes that the universe is composed of mass–energy, and that this is all that is real.

Physics Science dealing with the properties of energy and matter and the relationships between them.

Physiology Science concerned with the function of organisms.

Pseudochromasthesia A near relative of genuine synaesthesia in which the words acquire colour associations through learning.

Psychology The study of human behaviour.

Psychometric The measurement of the unobservable characteristics of living organisms.

Qualitative Concerned with distinctions based on qualities.

Quantitative Concerned with distinctions made on quantities.

rCBF Regional cerebral blood flow.

Recessive A genetic disorder that appears only in patients who have received two copies of a mutant gene, one from each parent.

Reliability As applied to psychological tests, how consistently the test measures an ability across time.

Res cognitans Mental material.

Res extensor Physical material.

SEP Somatosensory evoked potentials.

SPECT Single photon emission computerized tomography.

Sensational Of the senses.

Sequelae Complications of a disease.

Standard deviation Statistical construct given by the equation: [*equation to be included*]Where s is standard deviation, N is the number of datum, x_i is each individual measurement, and x *bar* is the mean of all measurements.

Substantia nigra Brain structure, damage to which can give rise to Parkinson's disease.

Synaesthesia Condition in which stimulation in one sensory modality gives rise to an involuntary sensation in another.

Synaesthesiae The percepts experienced by individuals with synaesthesia.

Synaesthete Individual with synaesthesia.

Thalamus Highly interconnected brain structure.

TMS Transcranial magnetic stimulation.

VEP Visually evoked potentials.

WAIS-R Wechsler adult intelligence scale (revised).

WMS-R Wechsler memory scale (revised).

Wernicke's area Brain region supposed by Carl Wernicke to be the neural substrate of speech production.

Within design An experimental design that relies upon comparing the performance of the same individuals on different occasions.

Further reading

Baron-Cohen, S., and Harrison, J. E. (1996) *Synaesthesia: classic and contemporary readings.* Oxford, Blackwell.

Cytowic, R. E. (1989) *Synesthesia: a union of the senses (Springer series in neuropsychology).* Springer.

Cytowic, R. E. (1995) *The man who tasted shapes.* Warner Books.

Nagel, T. (1974) What is it like to be a bat? *The Philosophical Review* **LXXXIII**, 435–50.

Smith Churchland, P. (1986) *Neurophilosophy: toward a unified science of the mind/brain.* MIT Press.

Zeki, S. (1993) *A vision of the brain.* Blackwell Science Inc.

References

Baron-Cohen, S., Wyke, M. and Binnie, C. (1987) Hearing words and seeing colours: an experimental investigation of synaesthesia. *Perception* **16**, 761–7.

Baron-Cohen, S., Harrison, J.E., Goldstein, L.H. and Wyke, M. (1993) Coloured speech perception: is synaesthesia what happens when modularity breaks down? *Perception* **22**, 419–26.

Baron-Cohen, S. and Harrison, J.E. (1996) *Synaesthesia: classic and contemporary readings.* Oxford, Blackwell.

Baron-Cohen, S. Burt, L., Smith-Laittan, F., Harrison, J.E. and Bolton, P. (1996) Synaesthesia: Prevalence and familiality. *Perception* 25(9),1073–9.

Baudelaire, C. (1860) *Les Paradis artificiels.* Paris: Gallimard.

Bender, M.B., Rudolph, S. and Stacey, C. (1982) The neurology of visual and oculomotor systems. In *Clinical Neurology.* Hagerstown, Harper and Row.

Bransford, J.D., Johnson, M.K. (1972) Contextual prerequisites for understanding: Some investigations of comprehension and recall. *Journal of Verbal learning and Verbal Behaviour* 11, 717–726.

Bücje, C., Price, C., Frackowiak, R.S.J. and Frith, C. (1998) Different activation patterns in the visual cortex of late and congenitally blind subjects. *Brain* 121(3), 409–19.

Byatt, A.S. (1985) *Still Life.* London, Penguin Books.

Calkins, M.W. (1893) A statistical study of pseudochromesthesia and of mental forms. *American Journal of Psychology* 5, 439–64.

Calkins, M.W. (1895) Synaesthesia. *American Journal of Psychology* 7, 90–107.

Chomsky, N. (1957) *Syntactic Structures.* The Hague, Mouton Publishers.

Churchland, P.S. (1986) *Neurophilosophy.* Cambridge MA, MIT Press.

Coriat, I.H. (1913a) A case of synaesthesia. *Journal of Abnormal Psychology* 8, 38–43.

Coriat, I.H. (193b) An unusual case of synaesthesia. *Journal of Abnormal Psychology* 8, 109–12.

Cytowic, R.E. and Wood, F.B. (1982) Synesthesia. II. Psychophysical relations in the synesthesia of geometrically shaped taste and colored hearing. *Brain and Cognition* 1(1), 36–49.

Cytowic, R.E. (1989) *Synesthesia: a union of the senses.* New York, Springer.

Cytowic, R.E. (1993) *The man who tasted shapes.* London, Abacus Books.

Downey, J.E. (1911) A case of colored gustation. *American Journal of Psychology* 22, 529–39.

Feynman, R.P. (1988) *What do you care what other people think?* London, HarperCollins.

Galton, F. (1883) *Inquiries into Human Faculty and its Development.* London: Dent.

Graziano, M.S.A., Yap, G.S., and Gross, C.G. (1994) Coding of visual space by premotor neurons. *Science* 266 (5187) 1054–7.

Hadjikhani, N., Liu, A.K., Dale, A.M., Cavanagh, P. and Tootell, R.B.H. (1998) Retinotopy and colour sensitivity in human visual cortical area V8. *Nature Neuroscience* 1(3), 235–41.

Halligan, P.W., Marshall, J.C., Hunt, M., and Wade, D.T. (1997) Somatosensory assessment: can seeing produce feeling? Journal of Neurology 244(3), 199–203.

Harrison, J. and Baron-Cohen, S. (1995) Synaesthesia: reconciling the subjective with the objective. *Endeavour* 19(4), 157–60.

Harrison, J.E. and Baron-Cohen, S.B. (1996) Acquired and inherited forms of cross-modal correspondence. *Neurocase* 2, 245–9.

Huysman, J.K. (1884) *Against Nature.* Paris, Cres; Penguin Books Trans. Robert Baldick (1959), London: Penguin.

Jacobs, L. Karpik, A., Bozian, D. and Gothgen, S. (1981) Auditory-visual synaesthesia: sound induced photisms. *Archives of Neurology* **38**, 211–16.

Krohn, W.O. (1893) Pseudo-chromesthesia, or the association of colours, with words, leters and sounds. *American Journal of Psychology* **5**, 20–39.

Lemley, B. (1999) Do you see what they see? *Discover* **20**(12), 23–4.

Lessell, S. and Cohen, M.M. (1979) Phosphenes induced by sound. *Neurology* **29**(11), 1524–6.

Locke, J. (1690) *An essay concerning human understanding: Book 3.* London: Basset; reprinted Oxford: Clarendon Press (1984).

Luria, A. (1968) *The mind of a mnemonist.* New York: Basic Books.

Marks, L. (1975) On coloured- hearing synaesthesia: cross-modal translations of sensory dimensions. *Psychological Bulletin* **82**(3), 303–31.

Merleau-Ponty, M. (1962) *Phenomenology of perception.* Hillsdale NJ, Humanities Press.

McKane, J.P. and Hughes, A.M. (1988) Synaesthesia and major affective disorder. *Acta Psychiatrica Scandinavica* **77**(4), 493–4.

Myers, C.S. (1915) Two cases of synaesthesia. *British Journal of Psychology* **7**, 112–17.

Nabokov, V. (1966) *Speak, memory.* London: Penguin.

Nagel, T. (1974) What is it like to be a bat? *The Philosophical Review* **LXXXIII**, 435–50.

Odin, S. (1986) Blossom scents take up the ringing: synaesthesia in Japanese and Western aesthetics. *Soundings* 69, 256–81.

Paulesu, E., Harrison, J.E., Baron-Cohen, S. Watson, J., Goldstein, L. Heather, J., Frackowiak, R. and Frith, C. (1995) The physiology of coloured hearing. *Brain* 118, 671–6.

Rizzo, M. and Eslinger, P.J. (1989) Colored hearing synesthesia: an investigation of neural factors. *Neurology* 39(6), 781–4.

Sadato, N., Pascual-Leone, A., Grafman, J., Ibanez, V., Deiber, M.P., Dold, G. and Hallett, M. (1996) Activation of the primary visual cortex by Braille reading in blind subjects. *Nature* 380(6574), 526–8.

Schiltz, K., Trocha, K., Wieringa, B.M., Emrich, H.M., Johannes, S., Munte, T.F. (1999) Neurophysiological aspects of synesthetic experience. *Journal of Neuropsychiatry & Clinical Neuroscience* 11(1), 58–65.

Skinner, B.F. (1957) *Verbal behaviour.* New York, Appleton-Century-Crofts.

Starr, F. (1893) Note on color hearing. *American Journal of Psychology* 51, 416–18.

Vike, J., Jabbari, B. and Maitland, C.G. (1984) Auditory-visual synesthesia. Report of a case with intact visual pathways. *Archives of Neurology* 41(6), 680–1.

Walsh, V. (1996) Perception: the seeing ear. *Current Biology* 6(4), 389–91.

Weber, E. (1986) *France fin de siècle.* London, Belknap Press.

Zeki, S. (1993) *A vision of the brain.* Oxford, Blackwell Science.

Zellner, D.A. and Kautz, M.A. (1990) Color affects perceived odour intensity. *Journal of Experimental Psychology* **16**(2), 391–7.

Index

Please note that page numbers that appear in **bold** represent a more major part of the text for that topic